BEING TRANSGENDER IN AMERICA

BY DUCHESS HARRIS, JD, PHD

WITH KRISTIN MARCINIAK

CONTENT CONSULTANT

HEATH FOGG DAVIS, PHD
DIRECTOR, GENDER, SEXUALITY,
AND WOMEN'S STUDIES PROGRAM
TEMPLE UNIVERSITY

Essential Library

An Imprint of Abdo Publishing | abdobooks.com

ABDOBOOKS.COM

Published by Abdo Publishing, a division of ABDO, PO Box 398166, Minneapolis, Minnesota 55439. Copyright © 2020 by Abdo Consulting Group, Inc. International copyrights reserved in all countries. No part of this book may be reproduced in any form without written permission from the publisher. Essential Library™ is a trademark and logo of Abdo Publishing.

Printed in the United States of America, North Mankato, Minnesota.
022019
092019

Cover Photo: iStockphoto
Interior Photos: Luiz Rampelotto/EuropaNewswire/Sipa/AP Images, 4–5; Monkey Business Images/Shutterstock Images, 7, 69; Shutterstock Images, 12, 17, 88–89; Africa Studio/Shutterstock Images, 15; Chelsea Guglielmino/Getty Images Entertainment/Getty Images, 20; Andrey Popov/Shutterstock Images, 23; Lynn Johnson/National Geographic, 27; Srdjan Randjelovic/Shutterstock Images, 30; Jeff Rayner/Barcroft USA/Barcroft Media/Getty Images, 32; iStockphoto, 36; Justin Starr Photography/Shutterstock Images, 38–39; John Tlumacki/The Boston Globe/ Getty Images, 42; Mark Reinstein/Shutterstock Images, 46; Geartooth Productions/ Shutterstock Images, 51; Dmytro Zinkevych/Shutterstock Images, 53; Red Line Editorial, 57; Lynne Sladky/AP Images, 60; Filipe Frazao/Shutterstock Images, 63; Erik McGregor/Sipa/AP Images, 66; Roy Rochlin/FilmMagic/Getty Images, 73; Netflix/Photofest, 77; FX Network/Photofest, 80; Yuchen Liao/Getty Images Entertainment/Getty Images, 82; Chris Young/The Canadian Press/AP Photo, 84; Craig Barritt/Shorty Awards/Getty Images Entertainment/Getty Images, 87; Little Pig Studio/Shutterstock Images, 94; Elaine Thompson/AP Images, 96; Christopher Penler/Shutterstock Images, 98

Editor: Megan Ellis
Series Designer: Melissa Martin

LIBRARY OF CONGRESS CONTROL NUMBER: 2018966009

PUBLISHER'S CATALOGING-IN-PUBLICATION DATA

Names: Harris, Duchess, author | Marciniak, Kristin, author.
Title: Being transgender in America / by Duchess Harris and Kristin Marciniak.
Description: Minneapolis, Minnesota : Abdo Publishing, 2020 | Series: Being LGBTQ in America | Includes online resources and index.
Identifiers: ISBN 9781532119033 (lib. bdg.) | ISBN 9781532173219 (ebook)
Subjects: LCSH: LGBTQ people--Juvenile literature. | Transgender identity--Juvenile literature. | Gender identity--United States--Juvenile literature. | Gender nonconformity--Juvenile literature.
Classification: DDC 306.768--dc23

CONTENTS

1

INTRODUCING
JAZZ

Fourteen-year-old Jazz Jennings hosts a sleepover with four of her friends. As her twin brothers lurk outside the door with cans of Silly String, Jennings and her friends crowd onto her bed for some girl talk. A television camera crew records every word. The teens discuss the social status that comes along with developing "boobs and butts."[1]

Like many teenagers, Jennings has insecurities about her body. She is particularly concerned with how people view her petite frame. Other girls in her grade believe "bigger is better" when it comes to breasts, but not Jennings. She would settle for breasts of any size. She says, "If I have boobs, then I could look like a girl to everyone else."[2]

Jennings is transgender, or trans. That means her gender identity is different from the sex assigned to her

Pronouns replace nouns in speech and writing. Using them is a good way to make sure a proper noun isn't repeated over and over again. In conversations, this includes people's names. Instead of repeating a person's name over and over, we often replace the name with gendered pronouns such as *he*, *she*, and *they*. Pronouns are also useful for confirming a trans person's gender identity. Using the correct pronoun for a trans person shows an understanding of who they are and how they would like to be addressed.

According to the Human Rights Campaign (HRC), the best rule of thumb is to use the pronoun that most closely aligns with how the subject of the conversation lives publicly. Jennings has always identified as female and wanted to live her life that way, which is why this book always uses *she* and *her*, even when talking about Jennings before she socially transitioned.

Some people in the transgender community identify with a gender that falls somewhere in between or outside the binary labels of *male* and *female*. They may also choose to identify as agender, or genderless. They may use pronouns such as *they* or *xir*. Unsure of which to use? The easiest way to clarify a person's pronouns is by asking the person politely.

at birth. More simply, as six-year-old Jennings told newswoman Barbara Walters in 2007, she was born with "a girl brain and a boy body."[3] Ever since she was little, all Jennings has wanted is a physical appearance that matches the way she feels inside.

GIRL IN TRANSITION

At birth, Jennings was given the name Jaron and assigned a sex of male. Despite this, Jennings was never confused about her gender, as some critics argue about trans people. She knew she was a girl, and she was desperate to look like one. At two years old, she dreamed about a "Good Fairy" who "promised to use her wand to turn [Jennings's] penis into a vagina."[4] Jennings was ecstatic about the dream. She really thought a fairy was going to change her body into the one she was meant to have.

Jennings's parents had some concerns about her desire to change her body. Then they met with therapists and doctors who helped them understand their child's gender dysphoria. Gender dysphoria is mental distress caused by a conflict between a person's assigned sex and their perception of their

As children get older, they may express their gender identity through their clothing preferences or the toys they like to play with.

own gender. Symptoms include depression, anxiety, and severe stress about one's body and assigned sex. Jennings's parents allowed her to live like a girl at home when she was three years old. Though her family still referred to her by male pronouns, Jennings wore dresses as she sang and danced her way around the house.

Being in public was a different matter. Jennings's dad was convinced that her gender identity was just a phase. He refused to leave the house with Jennings if she was dressed in feminine clothing. "I just was in denial," he recounted in the first episode of the family's reality show, *I Am Jazz*.[5] He thought Jennings would identify more as a boy as she got older.

However, Jennings's insistence that she was female only grew stronger over time. The happy little girl whom her parents saw at home was miserable when she couldn't express her gender correctly in public. This included wearing what society says are girls' clothes. At only four years old, Jennings felt many negative emotions while hiding her gender identity. These included loneliness, anger, jealousy, and frustration. Jennings's parents were unable to watch her suffer any longer. They agreed to help her transition to expressing her identity full time.

Jennings's unofficial coming out took place at her fifth birthday party. She spent the day eating snow cones. She raced down an inflatable water slide in a sparkly rainbow one-piece bathing suit. Jennings shared the day with family and friends. "It was the happiest day of the first five years of my life," Jennings wrote in her 2016 memoir, *Being Jazz: My Life as a (Transgender) Teen*.[6] Everyone could finally see what she knew all along—she was a girl.

IN THE SPOTLIGHT

The Jennings family gained national attention in 2007 when they were interviewed by Barbara Walters for her *20/20* news program. At the time, trans children and their families did not speak publicly. Many were afraid of harassment and discrimination. However, Jennings's parents knew a nationally broadcast interview could educate many viewers about trans people. They agreed to an interview with Walters. She had frank conversations with Jennings about being

BALANCING THE PUBLIC AND PRIVATE

The Jennings family was concerned about privacy when they shared their story. Like any family, they did not want negative commentary or vicious threats to disrupt their lives. Even on their reality show, the family does not talk about where they live. They also use pseudonyms, or fake names. Jennings is not the family's real last name. "Jazz" was originally a pseudonym that Jennings chose for her first interview with Barbara Walters. However, the name stuck. She began using it full time at the end of elementary school.

a trans child. She also asked Jennings's parents what it was like to raise a trans child.

The family received thank-you letters from trans children and their families after the episode aired. According to Jennings, the letter writers "no longer felt alone in what they were going through."[7] Jennings and her parents agreed to other interviews over the years. In 2011, the documentary *I Am Jazz: A Family in Transition* aired on television. Four years later, *I Am Jazz* became a reality show. Jennings became one of the most visible young trans people in popular culture.

MORE TEENS IDENTIFYING AS TRANS

Based on a 2016 survey of ninth and eleventh graders in Minnesota, researchers at the University of Minnesota estimate that 3 percent of teenagers nationwide identify as "transgender" or "other gender."[8] Just a year earlier, the University of California, Los Angeles (UCLA), estimated it was only 0.7 percent.[9] However, this doesn't necessarily mean there are more trans teens than ever before. Some experts believe the growing visibility of young trans people has made other teens feel comfortable expressing their gender identity openly.

THE ROAD AHEAD

As of 2018, Jazz Jennings is just like any other teenager—or at least one with her own reality television series and a popular YouTube channel. She loves playing sports, going to the beach, drawing, and hanging out with her friends and family. Like everyone else, she worries about school, how she looks, and what potential romantic interests think of her.

However, Jennings has also faced challenges most of her peers rarely have to consider. For example, the administrators at her elementary school refused to let Jennings use the girls' restroom. She had to use the bathroom in the nurse's office instead. And when she was in third grade, the Florida Youth Soccer Association barred her from playing on a girls' travel soccer team. It said she had the "unfair advantage" of having been "born in a boy's body."[10] The experience was isolating and frustrating for Jennings. In the end, the US Soccer Federation created a policy that allows players to play for the team that best matches their gender identity. Jennings was able to return to the girls' team.

THE FAMILY FOUNDATION

Before Jazz transitioned, her parents spent hours scouring the internet for resources and support groups. They were looking for guidance about raising a transgender child, but there was not a lot of information online. Because of this, the Jennings family and the parents of another trans child started the TransKids Purple Rainbow Foundation (TKPRF), a nonprofit organization that supports trans children and their families. A big component of that support is educating schools and communities. The organization hopes to decrease the stigma associated with being trans. Today TKPRF is run by the Jennings family with a therapist specializing in sex and gender.

Being a trans person in the United States isn't easy. Trans people contend with discrimination that puts their health, happiness, and safety at risk. Historically, society in the United States has favored people who are cisgender (cis), meaning

Sports teams are often separated by gender. This can affect trans people, who may be forced to play on a sports team as their assigned sex.

their gender identity matches the sex they were assigned at birth. This has led to discrimination in health care, education, employment, and housing practices for trans people. Trans people have high rates of poverty and homelessness. They also have an alarmingly high risk of being victims of violence and suicide when compared with cis people.

Advocacy groups such as the National Center for Transgender Equality (NCTE) and the Transgender Law Center work at the local, state, and national levels to end discrimination by changing government policy. People such as Jennings and her parents are also doing their part. They believe the best way to achieve acceptance and equality is to live openly and unapologetically. For the Jenningses, this means sharing parts of their lives with camera crews and YouTube fans. As Jennings wrote in her memoir, "Change happens through understanding."[11] For trans people searching for acceptance, societal understanding can't come a moment too soon.

DISCUSSION STARTERS

- If you had a story similar to Jazz Jennings's, would you share it? Why or why not? What if you thought sharing it would help other people?

- Do you think young children are capable of understanding their gender identity? Why or why not?

- How might Jennings's fame help her connect to other trans people and their families? How might it distance her from them?

2

WHAT DOES IT MEAN TO BE TRANSGENDER?

Someone who is transgender identifies with a different gender than the sex assigned to them at birth. Medical professionals determine sex based on a baby's genitalia. They decide that babies born with penises are boys, those with vulvas are girls, and those with atypical genitalia are intersex.

One's external genitalia and one's inner sense of self don't always match. According to estimates by the Williams Institute at the UCLA School of Law, there are approximately 1.4 million transgender people in the United States. That's about 0.6 percent of the country's adult population.[1] However, not all trans people are the same. *Transgender* and *trans* are used as umbrella terms, or cultural labels, to describe many different gender identities.

BEYOND THE BINARY

Many people view gender as a binary of male or female, or limited to only two genders. However, gender is a spectrum. Male is at one end and female at the other end. Cis men, cis women, trans men, and trans women have gender identities that align with male and female. Their gender expressions, or the way they present themselves, may or may not align with masculinity or femininity.

Some people have gender identities that are neither male nor female. These identities fall somewhere along the spectrum. These identities may also shift over time. People within this group may refer to themselves as nonbinary, genderfluid, or genderqueer. They may use pronouns such as *they* or *xir*. They may also use multiple sets of pronouns depending on the situation. "Growing up, I never felt people were *wrong* when they called me a woman, but it

ARE TRANSGENDER PEOPLE INTERSEX?

Being transgender is not the same as being intersex. Intersex people have reproductive anatomy that doesn't correspond to traditional ideas of male and female biology. For example, an intersex person may be born with female genitalia on the outside but have male organs on the inside. Intersex conditions are hormonal and chromosomal and may not be visible to the naked eye. Gender identity is an internal experience. Some intersex people identify as transgender, but not every intersex person is trans.

Some people express gender fluidity by wearing a variety of different types of clothing.

felt like a label imposed on me rather than one that fit," wrote Suzannah Weiss in a 2018 *Teen Vogue* article. "I don't want to identify with [the gender binary]."[2]

Weiss isn't alone. According to a survey by GLAAD, a group that studies and seeks to improve media coverage of LGBTQ issues, 20 percent of millennials identify as something other than straight and cisgender. This is compared to 7 percent of baby boomers. GLAAD president and chief executive officer Sarah Kate Ellis states that teenagers and young adults are "redefining everything" when it comes to gender.[3]

There are also people who identify as agender. They view themselves as being genderless, or without a gender to express. Mya, a teen who identifies as agender, gave an interview to *Teen Vogue* in 2016. Mya said, "Growing up, I never had that sense of being a guy, girl, or something else. My gender simply isn't there."[4]

WHEN DOES A PERSON KNOW THEY ARE TRANS?

There's no timeline for understanding one's sexuality or gender. For example, a person who initially feels an attraction to members of the opposite sex may later realize they are also attracted to members of the same sex. Likewise, not every transgender person has always known they were trans. Some people figure it out before they reach elementary school, but for others it may be a slow process that can take years or even decades.

HISTORICAL AND GLOBAL PERSPECTIVES

Having a gender identity that differs from the one assigned at birth is not a modern concept. Philo of Judea, a Jewish thinker in Ancient Greece, wrote about people in 30 BCE who would today be considered transgender. Historical documents indicate that the Roman emperor Elagabalus was assigned male at birth but ruled as a woman from 218 to 222 CE. Some historians wonder whether the Egyptian pharaoh Hatshepsut was transgender. She lived as a woman prior to taking the crown but presented herself as a man during most of her rule from 1479 to 1458 BCE. Artifacts found in her tomb depict her as a king, not a queen.

Today, trans people are found in every culture around the world. For example, many Native American tribes, including the Navajo, Zuni, and Lakota, believe there are more than two genders. In the 1990s, LGBTQ activists from many Native American nations created a term that would describe trans people across native tribes and cultures. After sharing information and teachings, the group decided on *two-spirit*. According to activist Beverly Little Thunder, a member of the Lakota people, "In many tribes if you are a two-spirit person, you embody both the masculine and the feminine."[5]

The Bugis people of Indonesia recognize five genders instead of two. Additionally, the Amhara people of Ethiopia acknowledge the existence of a third gender that is somewhere between male and female. Prior to the influence of white Europeans, the Dagaaba tribe of what is today Ghana, Burkina Faso, and the Ivory Coast believed gender was an energy, not a physical determination. According to Dagaaba shaman Malindoma Somé, "One who is physically male can vibrate female energy, and vice versa. That is where the real gender is."[6]

THE ROOTS OF GENDER IDENTITY

Scientists do not know why some people are transgender and some people are cisgender. For the first half of the 1900s, it

Two-spirit people come from many different Native American nations.

was widely believed that a person's biological sex, gender, and sexual orientation were all the same thing. That is now widely considered untrue. Just like cis people, trans people can have any sexuality. As genderfluid YouTube personality Brendan Jordan describes it, "Sexuality is who you go to bed with, and gender identity is who you go to bed *as*."[7]

In 1949, sexologist David O. Cauldwell published an article that said having a gender identity different from the one assigned at birth was a mental illness. Cauldwell was wrong—being transgender is not a mental illness. However, mental health providers used his theory for more than 50 years to pathologize trans people. Cauldwell's article is one of the reasons why there is still a negative stigma attached to trans people today. Between 1980 and 2012, the American Psychiatric Association (APA) maintained that all transgender people had gender identity disorder. The main symptom of this illness was a person's belief they were a gender other than the one they were assigned at birth. Because of this, many mental health providers sought to cure a person's gender identity.

Medical and psychological research has proven that gender identity isn't something that can be cured. It is simply part of who someone is. Even so, many transgender people experience feelings of distress about their gender and their bodies. The APA addressed this in the 2013 edition of the *Diagnostic and Statistical Manual of Mental Disorders* (*DSM*). Gender identity disorder was removed and a new condition, gender dysphoria, was added. Gender dysphoria is the stress a person experiences when their gender identity does not match the sex they were assigned at birth. This change in diagnosis and classification allows mental health professionals to treat the symptoms of gender dysphoria without trying to cure someone of their gender identity.

GENDER DYSPHORIA

Proponents of gender dysphoria's inclusion in the *DSM* say it helps trans people verify the realness of their gender identity and ensures they will get proper treatment for their dysphoria. But there are many people who feel the *DSM* listing does more harm than good. They argue it still positions all trans people as having a disease, dysfunction, or mental disorder, which can lead to negative stigmas and societal discrimination. For example, in March 2018, Defense Secretary Jim Mattis recommended that people with a history or diagnosis of gender dysphoria be barred from serving in the military because they "presen[t] considerable risk to military effectiveness and lethality."[8] Misconceptions like this often result in the loss of transgender people's civil rights.

BIOLOGICAL EVIDENCE

Other theories about why some people are trans and others aren't have been explored over the years. Most research about gender identity today focuses on the brain. One example is the bed nucleus of the stria terminalis (BSTc). It controls the involuntary responses of the central nervous system, such as anxiety. The BSTc is twice as large in cisgender men as in cisgender women.

Sexually dimorphic areas of the brain, or areas that are different between the sexes, are good points of comparison. Two studies, one in 1995 and one in 2000, independently discovered that transgender women had BSTcs that were closer in size and cell density to those of cisgender women than those of cisgender men. They found that trans men had BSTcs that were closer in size and cell density to those of cisgender men. Put simply, a transgender person's brain can match their gender identity while their body does not.

Subsequent studies confirming this theory led researchers to explore why some people's brains don't match the rest of their anatomy. No one has found a concrete answer yet. Some scientists think it has to do with the womb, where a lot of brain development occurs. It is thought that hormones

People who have gender dysphoria may discuss their feelings with mental health professionals.

in the mother's uterus, and the fetus's ability to receive those hormones, affect how the fetus's brain is structured. For example, female embryos are exposed to a little bit of testosterone, the male sex hormone, and a lot of estrogen, the female sex hormone. In most cases, the abundance of estrogen causes the fetus to develop a female-specific brain structure. But if that estrogen can't reach the fetus, either because there isn't enough in the womb or because the fetus isn't sensitive enough to it, then the fetus develops the brain structure associated with the male hormone. The baby is born with a male brain and a female body. Later, that person may identify as a trans man.

Though many in the scientific community are eager to learn more about the biological aspects of gender identity, some trans advocates aren't as enthusiastic. They worry

A CALL TO DE-EMPHASIZE MEDICAL RESEARCH

Biological research about gender identity is a fascinating topic, but some experts don't think it will positively change the way trans people are perceived and treated in US society. Samantha Allen has a PhD in women's, gender, and sexuality studies. In a 2018 opinion piece for the Daily Beast, she argued that people often overlook scientific evidence when it comes to forming opinions. Even if scientists prove there are genetic markers for being transgender, that doesn't mean trans people will be embraced by those who are prejudiced against them. "It doesn't matter what causes people to be transgender, it matters that they are supported," she wrote.[9]

finding a biological root of gender identity will lead to further discrimination. For example, a person who identifies as trans but lacks biological proof may not be granted the same civil rights. There are also concerns that communities that do not accept transgender people would try to fix those whose gender identity differs from their assigned sex.

Despite these fears, proponents of scientific research feel there is value to learning more about biology and gender identity, especially when it comes to providing medical care for the trans community. These efforts are still in the early stages. Researchers generally agree gender identity is rooted in biology. Like eye color and hair texture, it is simply part of who people are.

DISCUSSION STARTERS

- What does it mean to you when a person says they don't have a gender?

- How does a person's gender personally impact someone else?

- What do you think causes some societies to accept transgender people while other societies don't?

- What do you think acceptance of the trans community looks like?

3

EXPRESSING
GENDER IDENTITY

Many people who identify as transgender choose to have their gender expression, or how they present themselves to the world, match their gender identity, or how they feel on the inside. Each person's gender expression is made of many different parts, including clothing, hairstyle, hobbies, and behavior. The process of changing the way one looks in order to be perceived as a different gender, or no gender at all, is currently known as transitioning. Transitioning is different for everyone—there's no right or wrong way to do it. No matter what a person decides, transitioning is a deeply personal decision and experience that may involve others in the person's social circle. What works for one person may not be the best choice for another.

SOCIAL TRANSITIONS

A social transition is often the first step in aligning someone's gender expression and identity. Changes are usually cosmetic.

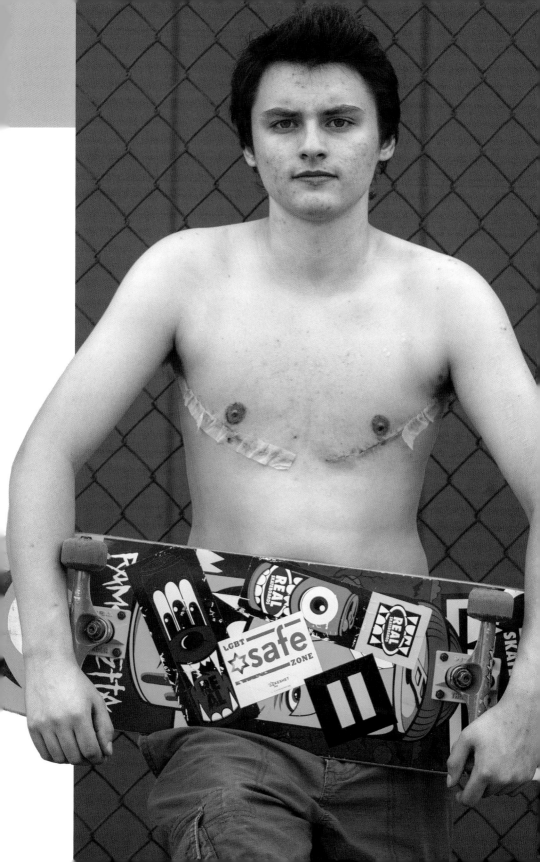

Trans women may grow out their hair, wear feminine clothing, and put on makeup. Some may choose to wear padded shapeware around the bust and hips to give the impression of a curvier body. Trans men may cut their hair short, opt for more masculine clothing, and wear compression bras or chest binders to flatten their breast tissue. A person who identifies as nonbinary may alternate between traditionally masculine and feminine clothing, hairstyles, and accessories.

A key component of social transition is coming out, or sharing one's gender identity with others. Some people may choose to come out at home, work, and school. Others may only feel comfortable being out with a specific group of supportive people. While the idea of coming out can be intimidating, the act itself can be an enormous relief. Staff Sergeant Ashleigh Buch of the US Air Force said that coming out felt like surfacing after a lifetime underwater. "It was just like that breath of fresh air," she said in an interview with Task & Purpose, a news website for military veterans. "It was like this weight was finally . . . lifted off my shoulders."[1]

Coming out also provides an opportunity to let people know about changes in pronouns, names, and personal behaviors. For example, an employee might inform their employer about their intention to use the bathroom that corresponds with their gender identity. Sharing this information helps family, friends, and coworkers understand how one wants to be perceived and treated.

HORMONE THERAPY

Some transgender people opt to receive medical procedures that change the physical appearance of their bodies. These alterations are often achieved by hormone therapy, surgery, or a combination of the two.

Hormones are chemicals that affect the growth and function of the human body. The hormones testosterone and estrogen are responsible for the secondary sex characteristics a person develops during puberty, such as breasts, widening hips and shoulders, and the appearance of facial and body hair. For many trans people, having the secondary sex characteristics of their assigned sex, or lacking the secondary sex characteristics of their preferred gender, causes

TRANSGENDER OR TRANSSEXUAL?

Transgender and *transsexual* are sometimes used interchangeably, but they also can mean two different things. *Transgender* describes a person who identifies with a gender other than the one they were assigned at birth. *Transsexual* usually describes a person who has had gender-affirming surgery or hormone replacement therapy (HRT). Some people consider the term *transsexual* to be outdated or even offensive. It may be a good idea to use *transgender* or *trans* unless someone specifically asks to be recognized as transsexual.

Hormones taken during HRT are often injected into the stomach, thighs, or glutes.

major distress. Other people make assumptions about gender based on these visual cues.

Trans patients can undergo hormone replacement therapy (HRT) under a doctor's supervision. Patients are given regular doses of the hormone that most closely matches their gender identity. In adults who have already completed puberty, this second puberty lessens the appearance of the previously developed traits. It also starts the development of traits that align with their gender identity. For example, trans women taking estrogen see the growth of breast tissue and a decrease in the thickness and growth rate of body hair. Some of their body fat is redistributed to the hips and thighs. Trans men who take testosterone become more muscular and their faces become more angular. Many develop facial hair, and some may stop menstruating. Nonbinary people may choose to take hormones to give themselves a more androgynous appearance. These results last as long as the hormones are taken regularly. However, some alterations from HRT are permanent. For example, testosterone can thicken the vocal chords and lower a person's voice. This cannot be changed if HRT is stopped.

Additionally, estrogen cannot make vocal chords thinner. People taking estrogen may also undergo speech therapy to pitch their voices higher. HRT may also lead to infertility.

Young transgender people who haven't gone through puberty may have the option of taking hormone blockers. Hormone blockers suppress naturally

PSYCHOLOGICAL BENEFITS OF HORMONE THERAPY

HRT doesn't just change a person's secondary sex characteristics. It also impacts mental health. In 2015, researchers at the Yale School of Public Health and Harvard Medical School analyzed three separate studies of transgender men and women in the early stages of HRT. Subjects self-assessed their mental states prior to HRT, after 3 to 6 months of HRT, and after 12 months of HRT. The researchers concluded HRT was related to a significant decrease in the subjects' rates of anxiety, depression, and other negative mental health symptoms. It also correlated with an increase in overall quality of life.[2]

occurring sex hormones. This prevents the development of secondary sex characteristics. They essentially pause puberty. Should the child or their family decide not to move forward with HRT, the blockers can be stopped. Naturally occurring puberty will resume. For many years, the Endocrine Society, a professional organization focused on the treatment of hormone disorders, recommended that children and teenagers wait to

Josie Romero, *center*, is a trans girl and the subject of the documentary *Aged 8 and Wanting a Sex Change*. Her family received criticism for starting her on hormone blockers at a young age.

pursue gender-affirming HRT until they are 16 years old. But many health-care providers and their trans patients elect to begin earlier. They prefer to base their timing on the patient's physical development. This was the case for Jazz Jennings. She started taking hormone blockers at 11 and had her first dose of estrogen at 12. Additionally, hormone blockers can be expensive, and parents need to research the topic heavily before deciding on a course of action for their child.

SURGICAL PROCEDURES

Some people who choose hormone therapy also opt for gender-affirming surgery. This means they have one or more surgical procedures that physically alter their bodies. The surgeries help their appearance match that of the gender with which they identify. Some of the most common surgeries are breast tissue implants, double mastectomies, vaginoplasty, and phalloplasty.

Trans people often refer to breast tissue implants and double mastectomies as "top" surgeries. Trans women may choose to have breast implants to increase the size of their breasts more than can be achieved through taking estrogen alone. Trans men who would rather have a flat, masculine chest may undergo a double mastectomy, which is the removal of breast tissue and mammary glands.

Vaginoplasty and phalloplasty are often referred to as "bottom" surgeries. In a vaginoplasty, which is performed on trans women, surgeons remove the patient's testicles and some structural parts of the penis. The urethra is shortened and rerouted to just outside the patient's new vagina, which is formed with either the skin of the former penis or a small part of the patient's large intestines. Phalloplasty, which is the surgical creation of a penis, is performed on trans men. Skin from the patient's arm or abdomen is rolled into the shape of a penis and stitched into place. Some trans men also choose to have their urethra lengthened and inserted into the new penis. Vaginoplasty, phalloplasty, and other bottom surgeries

THE DANISH GIRL

Lili Elbe was one of the first people in the world to undergo gender-affirming surgery. Elbe was a talented landscape artist who studied at the Royal Danish Academy of Fine Arts in the early 1900s. There she met her future wife, Gerda Gottlieb, who was a fashion illustrator and portrait artist.

Elbe's long-suppressed desire to experience life as a woman surfaced one day when Gottlieb asked Elbe to dress in women's clothing and pose for her. The couple soon moved to Paris, France. Because they knew no one there, Elbe could appear publicly as a man or a woman. Elbe began a series of surgical procedures to affirm her female identity in 1930. She died just a year later when her body rejected an experimental uterine transplant.

Elbe's story was first told in her book *Man into Woman: The First Sex Change*, which was published after her death. A fictionalized version of her story is told in the novel *The Danish Girl* by David Ebershoff, which was made into a movie in 2015.

are incredibly complex procedures. Unlike most top surgeries, they haven't yet been perfected. Fewer people choose to undergo bottom surgery because of the cost and uncertain outcomes.

Like all other aspects of transitioning, surgery is not for every person. Gender-affirming surgeries can be extremely expensive. Many types, particularly bottom surgeries, aren't covered by insurance companies. In many cases, that's because state laws do not require insurance providers to offer transition-related coverage. There's also the hardship of recovery, which can be long and painful. However, the decision to alter one's body is very personal. "I always felt that my body was an unfinished sculpture," said an anonymous trans man on *Cosmopolitan*'s website in 2016. "Once I chipped away the unnecessary parts, I felt more like myself."[3]

BEING A BETTER ALLY

Cisgender friends and family members may feel at a loss about how to talk to and support someone who has transitioned or is going through the process. Support network PFLAG offers a free online guidebook about how to be a good trans ally. In addition to providing definitions of commonly used terms, the *Guide to Being a Trans Ally* addresses common ally fears ("What if I say the wrong thing? Is it okay to ask about . . . ?") and suggests opportunities for further education about trans people and issues.

TRANSITIONING TO A HAPPIER, HEALTHIER LIFE

Whether medical intervention is involved or not, many transgender people find emotional and mental relief in being able to express their felt gender identities. A 2016 study published in the journal *Pediatrics* showed that trans children in supportive environments are less likely to suffer from depression and anxiety than those who don't transition. The same is true for adults, many of whom see the severity

Trans children who have support from their parents often have fewer issues with their mental health later in life.

of their gender dysphoria decrease or disappear entirely after transitioning.

Many mental health professionals even view medical transitions such as hormone therapy and gender-affirming surgeries as being medically necessary. According to online mental health directory GoodTherapy, all major psychological, psychiatric, and medical organizations in the United States agree that "aligning the physical body with internal identity can greatly relieve distress, mental health symptoms, and [risk of suicide]."[4] Blue Montana, a trans man interviewed by *U.S. News & World Report* in 2017, put the suicide risk more bluntly. "For a lot of us, transitioning saved our lives," he said. "If I didn't transition, I'd be dead."[5]

DISCUSSION STARTERS

- What is your gender identity? How do you express it?
- Why do you think people express their gender identities in different ways?
- What do you think defines a person's sex? Is it anatomy, hormones, feelings, or something else?

Trans people and their allies protest and march to advocate for equal rights.

LEGAL
CHALLENGES

Like other minority groups, trans people have often been the focus of legal and cultural discrimination. Implementing nationwide protections, such as federal voting-rights laws and the legalization of same-sex marriage, has traditionally been an important step in reducing bias in the United States. This has not yet happened for trans people. As of January 2019, no federal laws explicitly prohibit discrimination based on gender identity. The lack of federal legal protection extends into all aspects of life, including education, employment, housing, health care, and military service. It has even found its way into the bathroom.

PUBLIC BATHROOMS

In February 2016, the city council of Charlotte, North Carolina, approved a law that prevented businesses from discriminating against gay or transgender customers. The law said that transgender people could use public restrooms that most

closely matched their gender identity. Conservative lawmakers in the North Carolina state legislature didn't like this. They argued that allowing trans women into women's bathrooms and locker rooms would put women at risk of encountering sexual predators. Some people said cis men would dress in women's clothing, go into women's restrooms, and then assault women and children.

In March 2016, the North Carolina state legislature passed House Bill 2 (HB2). The bill prohibited cities from passing their own LGBTQ antidiscrimination laws. Instead, all local and city governments had to follow the state's antidiscrimination laws. The state's laws did not include protections for sexuality or gender identity. HB2 also said all people in North Carolina had to use the facilities that matched the gender on their birth certificates when at public schools and state agencies.

OPENLY TRANS POLITICIANS

In January 2018, former journalist Danica Roem became the first openly transgender state legislator in US history. Her 2017 campaign for a seat in Virginia's House of Delegates pitted her against sitting delegate Bob Marshall, a Republican who once sponsored a bill that would require trans people to use restrooms that corresponded to the gender on their birth certificates. In an interview with *Time* magazine, Roem said she hopes her election will spur other trans people to run for office "and get elected because of who they are, not despite it."[1] She and other trans advocates look forward to the day when a politician's values, ideas, and positions are more important than personal characteristics such as gender identity.

The backlash was immediate. The National Basketball Association (NBA) and National Collegiate Athletic Association (NCAA) moved games out of state. This cost North Carolina hundreds of millions of dollars in tourist revenue. The US Department of Justice sued North Carolina for violating the civil rights of transgender people. The US Department of Education threatened to withhold part of the state's $4 billion in federal funding for its schools.

In response, legislators replaced HB2 with House Bill 142 (HB142) in March 2017. HB142 removed the restrictions on bathroom usage. However, it purposefully excluded language regarding trans people using the bathroom of their choice. That means many trans people, including students, legally cannot use the bathrooms that match their gender identity. This type of "gender policing" also means cis people whose gender expression doesn't match society's binary expectations may not be able to use their bathroom of choice either. HB142 also says local governments can't make any laws about public bathrooms without the approval of the state legislature. Additionally, no citywide antidiscrimination laws can be made until December 2020.

The 2015 US Transgender Survey (USTS), which cataloged and analyzed the responses of nearly 28,000 transgender people in the United States and its territories, found that 26 percent of trans people were "denied access to restrooms,

Inclusive restrooms are easier for trans people to navigate when out in public.

had their presence in a restroom questioned, and/or were verbally harassed, physically attacked, or sexually assaulted in a restroom." It also found that more than one-half of the survey's respondents avoided using public restrooms out of fear for their own safety.[2] This can have damaging effects on a person's health. People may intentionally dehydrate themselves to avoid having to use public restrooms. Additionally, a person who waits too long to use the restroom may develop a urinary tract infection. Meanwhile, as of 2019, there have been zero documented instances of transgender people assaulting others in public restrooms.

SCHOOL SPORTS

One of the biggest questions that has come out of the increased visibility of the trans population is how to handle participation in gender-specific sports. For example, high school senior Mack Beggs is a trans boy who began taking testosterone at 15. He's also a two-time Texas girls' state wrestling champion.

Beggs loves to wrestle. It got him through a lot of hard times when he was coming to terms with his gender identity. After beginning HRT, he petitioned to be moved to the boys' division. The University Interscholastic League, which oversees high school sports in Texas, denied his request. Beggs had to compete in the division that matched his birth certificate, which said he was female.

Some coaches, parents, and female wrestlers complained that Beggs had an unfair advantage because of the HRT. Others said Beggs's success was the result of skill and training, not testosterone. Despite the controversy surrounding his

There's not a clear answer on whether schools like Mack Beggs's need to allow trans athletes to participate in the divisions that most closely match their gender identity. Many people look to Title IX of the Education Amendments of 1972 for guidance. It states that students cannot be excluded "on the basis of sex" from participation in any program or activity offered by schools or other organizations receiving money from the federal government.[4] At issue is the word *sex*. During President Barack Obama's administration, the Departments of Justice and Education interpreted the word *sex* to include a person's gender identity. That meant student athletes could play on the team that matched their gender identity. The Trump administration rescinded that guidance in early 2017. Secretary of Education Betsy DeVos has said it is up to state and local organizations to interpret the guidelines as they see fit.

participation in the girls' division, Beggs went undefeated in 2017 and 2018. In college, he wrestled in the men's division.

MILITARY SERVICE

In 2016, the US Department of Defense lifted a nearly 60-year ban on transgender people serving in the military. It was first instituted in the early 1960s when people still thought being transgender was a mental illness. However, this ban did not stop trans people who wanted to serve. According to a 2014 study by the Williams Institute, 21.4 percent of transgender people have served in the military. By comparison, less than 11 percent of all adults in the United States have served.[3] Researchers concluded that transgender people are more likely to join the military than the average adult in the United States, even when they have to hide who they are.

In June 2016, the Department of Defense under the Obama administration implemented a new policy that said trans soldiers already in the military could be open about their gender identification and transition without risk of dishonorable discharge. New recruits who openly identified as trans would be allowed to enlist starting January 1, 2018. That policy came under attack in July 2017. President Donald Trump announced via Twitter that "the United States Government will not accept or allow transgender individuals to serve in any capacity in the U.S. Military."[5] A month later, Trump formally ordered the Department of Defense to reverse the 2016 policy.

Public reaction was swift. Individual trans soldiers sued the US government for the right to serve openly in the military. Four federal courts said the government couldn't enforce the ban until those court cases were concluded. Because of that, the US government was forced to accept new transgender military recruits at the beginning of 2018 as previously planned.

Trump issued a new memo in March 2018 that stated "transgender persons with a history or diagnosis of gender dysphoria . . . are disqualified from military service except under certain limited circumstances."[6] Exceptions would be made for people who identify as transgender but have not transitioned, those who are diagnosed with gender dysphoria while enlisted and do not transition, and those who have transitioned and are already enlisted.

Trump issued an order in 2018 that disqualified transgender people from enlisting in the military.

In January 2019, the Supreme Court ruled that the ban on transgender service members could remain in place while the cases about the ban went through the federal court system. This meant that transgender servicepeople were at risk of being discharged from military service due to their gender identity. Additionally, trans people who were not already in the military before the ban went into effect would not be able to join the military.

IDENTIFICATION DOCUMENTS

Government-issued identification documents (IDs) verify a person's very existence. One of the biggest legal struggles for many trans people is changing the gender marker on their IDs.

A government-issued ID is mandatory for many basic activities. These include traveling, voting, driving, attending school, and applying for a credit card. Some examples of IDs are passports, birth certificates, and drivers' licenses. Most employers need copies of their employees' IDs. Some states require copies of a couple's birth certificates to certify a marriage. Having an ID that lists the wrong gender raises suspicion about one's true identity, which can lead to a denial of services or the involvement of law enforcement.

WHAT'S IN A NAME?

Legally changing one's name is generally much easier than changing a gender marker. Yet for some trans people, changing their names can be dangerous. As of 2017, more than a dozen states require name-change applicants to publish their new names in local newspapers anywhere from two to four times over the course of several weeks.[7] This type of public "outing" puts trans people at risk of violence and harassment. Some states, including Indiana and Ohio, waive the publishing requirement for situations in which a person's safety might be compromised.

Not having IDs that match one's gender identity can make trans people feel isolated and misunderstood. It can also cause humiliation and psychological distress. It may even lead to acts of harassment and violence from people who notice the discrepancy between the ID and the person's gender expression. People who would otherwise not be perceived as trans are at risk every time they hand over their IDs to a stranger, such as when going through airport security.

GENDER MARKER X

Driver's license gender markers—*M* for male and *F* for female—assume that everyone has a binary gender identity. That's not the case. Many trans, nonbinary, and agender people don't feel comfortable with having either of those gender markers on their driver's licenses or state-issued IDs. That's why as of January 2019, some states, including Arkansas, California, Maine, Minnesota, Oregon, and Washington, as well as Washington, DC, offer a third gender option: *X*. In most cases, a doctor's note is not required. Additional gender markers not only provide a more accurate representation of the ID's owner but also offer a sense of privacy for those who don't wish to share their gender identity with strangers.

It is possible to change the gender marker on most forms of IDs. However, the process can be expensive and difficult. Federal documents generally require a physician's certification of a person's transition. The procedures and costs associated with altering birth certificates, drivers' licenses, and other state IDs depend on the state of issuance. For example, Colorado only requires a written statement from the person's physician verifying the transition. But in Louisiana, trans people can't change the marker on their birth certificates unless they have had gender-affirming surgery. That means people who decide not to surgically transition, or who can't afford it, can't change the gender identity listed on their state-issued IDs. In Iowa, changing gender markers requires both surgery and a court order from a judge. As of February 2019, three states—Kansas, Ohio, and Tennessee—would not reissue birth certificates with the correct gender.

One-third of trans people who have socially transitioned have not been able to change any of their IDs. This might be because a person's situation doesn't match their state's requirements (for example, they haven't had gender-affirming surgery), because of the cost, or because they don't have the correct medical documentation. In all, only 21 percent of transgender people have been able to successfully update all forms of their IDs.[8] That leaves the rest at risk for hassle, harassment, and unnecessary hardships.

DISCUSSION STARTERS

- Why do you think some people try to prevent trans people from using the restrooms that align with their gender identity?

- Not everyone identifies as male or female. How do ID laws affect nonbinary people? How could states make IDs more inclusive?

5

Trans people may feel unsafe being open in the workplace about their gender identity.

ECONOMIC
CHALLENGES

Only a few federal laws prevent institutions from denying someone an equal education, job opportunities, housing, or even health care because of their gender identity. Washington, DC, and fewer than half of the 50 states have adopted trans-inclusive laws.[1] This has major economic consequences for members of the transgender community. According to the 2015 USTS, 29 percent of transgender people in the United States live in poverty.[2] That means they earn less than $11,770 per year.[3] For comparison, the poverty rate for the entire US population at the time of the survey was 12 percent.[4]

BULLYING

One of the biggest problems facing trans students at school is bullying. The 2015 National Transgender Discrimination Survey revealed that 54 percent of trans students have been verbally harassed at school. Almost 25 percent have been physically

attacked, and 13 percent have been sexually assaulted. More than one-third of trans students have been disciplined for fighting back against bullies. Trans students are five times more likely than their cisgender peers to miss school because of fear of harassment. Students who are chronically absent and miss more than ten days of school per year have a much higher dropout rate than students who attend school regularly.[5]

Discrimination can also impact trans students' access to a safe and comfortable learning environment. Joel Baum, the senior director of professional development at Gender Spectrum, an organization dedicated to gender inclusion, said discriminatory policies send trans students "a chilling message. . . . You are not who you think you are, and we do not endorse who you are at all."[7]

TRANS-INCLUSIVE POLICIES AT SINGLE-SEX COLLEGES

In 2014, all-female Mills College announced a change to its admission procedures. Breaking the long-standing tradition of admitting only cisgender females, the Oakland, California, school opened admissions to include trans women, trans men who are still legally considered female, and nonbinary students who are legally considered female. Other all-women's colleges soon followed suit. By 2017, 26 out of the 39 major all-women's colleges in the United States had admitted some trans students, though the policies and numbers varied by institution.[6] In contrast, there are only 3 men's colleges in the United States. Only one college, Morehouse, has mentioned the enrollment of trans students.

Trans students may be bullied in school because of their gender identity.

According to the 2015 National School Climate Survey, 60 percent of transgender students were required to use a restroom or locker room that did not match their gender identity. Nearly 51 percent weren't allowed to use their preferred name or pronouns, and 22.2 percent were prohibited from expressing their gender through their clothing.[8] As of January 2019, only 17 states and Washington, DC, explicitly prohibited discrimination based on gender identity in an educational setting.

EMPLOYMENT

Transgender people are also at a greater risk for discrimination in the workforce. As of February 2019, only 21 states

INTERPRETING THE LAW

Most workers in the United States are protected from employment discrimination by Title VII of the Civil Rights Act of 1964. It prohibits workplace discrimination based on "race, color, religion, sex, or national origin."[10] There is no explicit mention of discrimination based on a person's gender identity.

This omission has caused a lot of debate about the rights of transgender people in the workforce. Some groups, including the Equal Employment Opportunity Commission (EEOC), which oversees the enforcement of Title VII, believe the law does protect trans employees. According to the EEOC, "sex discrimination includes discrimination based on an applicant or employee's gender identity or sexual orientation."[11]

However, former attorney general Jeff Sessions came out with a new directive in October 2017. He argued the word *sex* in Title VII refers only to "discrimination between men and women [but not] discrimination based on gender identity . . . including transgender status."[12] Based on that point of view, it is legal to deny an employee a job or promotion because of their gender identity.

and Washington, DC, had laws that explicitly prohibited employment discrimination based on gender identity.[9] Trans people can be fired, denied promotions, or miss out on job opportunities because of their gender identity or expression. That's what happened to Aimee Stephens. In 2013, she was fired from her job two weeks after informing her boss about her transition. Luckily, Stephens found a new job that accepted her.

Other trans workers aren't so lucky. Fifteen percent of trans people in the workforce experienced verbal harassment, physical attacks, or sexual assaults while on the job.[13]

Discrimination forces some trans people into taking jobs for which they are overqualified. Many others can't find work. In 2015, the transgender community's 15 percent unemployment rate was three times higher than the national average.[14]

Lack of adequate employment and compensation puts members of the transgender community at a higher risk for poverty and homelessness. Twenty percent of respondents in the 2015 USTS reported engaging in underground economies, such as selling drugs and doing sex work, to make ends meet. "I couldn't find work," an anonymous survey respondent wrote. "I watched one guy throw away my application literally 30 seconds after turning it in. I resorted to escorting. It's the only way to keep food in my belly and a roof over my head."[15]

But as time goes on, more and more employers are becoming accepting and supportive of their trans employees. Cass Averill, a computer security specialist from Eugene, Oregon, came out to his employer after two years on the job. The Fortune 500 company for which he worked didn't have any policies in place for trans employees. Averill's manager became his biggest ally. "The acceptance received while transitioning on the job directly impacted my confidence and helped me find my voice," Averill wrote in a 2015 opinion piece for the *New York Times*.[16] He has since become an advocate for the LGBTQ community.

STATE BY STATE

As of 2018, the federal government had left it up to individual states to decide how and when to extend civil rights to transgender people. California, Vermont, Washington, Oregon, and Colorado have been the most progressive when it comes to trans rights. These states offered their trans residents explicit protections in everything from housing to employment to health care. In 2015, digital media company Refinery29 named those five states the best places for trans people to live.

The Southeast, the Mideast, the upper Western mountain territories, and parts of the Midwest of the United States have few to no legal protections for trans people. This means people can deny someone a promotion or a home loan because of their gender identity. It is also legal to deny students their right to attend school as their preferred gender. Additionally, Arizona, Oklahoma, Texas, Louisiana, Alabama, Mississippi, and South Carolina restrict schools from teaching some LGBTQ topics. South Dakota and Missouri have laws that prevent school districts from specifically protecting LGBTQ students.

This US map shows state-by-state protections and restrictions based on gender identity as of December 2018.

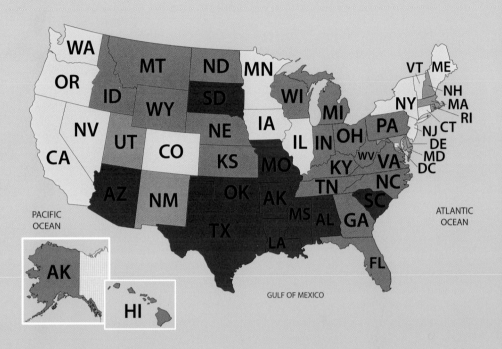

WA

OR

MT

ID

WY

NV

UT

CA

AZ

ND

SD

NE

CO

NM

MN

WI

IA

KS

OK

TX

MI

IL

IN

MO

AK

MS

LA

OH

KY

TN

AL

GA

WV

VT

NY

PA

NJ

DE

VA

NC

SC

FL

ME

NH

MA

RI

CT

MD

DC

PACIFIC
OCEAN

ATLANTIC
OCEAN

AK

HI

GULF OF MEXICO

Education Restrictions

Minor or No Explicit Legal Protections

Employment and Housing Protections

Employment, Housing, and Education Protections

HOUSING

As of 2018, there are no federal housing laws that specifically protect transgender home buyers, homeowners, or renters. In many parts of the country, a landlord can evict a tenant for being transgender. A landlord can also refuse them housing in the first place. Lenders can even deny an applicant's loan based on gender identity.

According to the 2015 USTS, 6 percent of transgender people were denied the rental or purchase of a home or apartment in 2015, while 5 percent were evicted from their place of residence because of their gender identity.[17] This type of discrimination forces many transgender people to take whatever housing they can get.

SEEKING SAFE HOMELESS SHELTERS

Finding a safe place to stay can be difficult for homeless trans people. Some shelters and agencies deny services to trans people because of misconceptions about gender identity. Organizations may also group overnight clients by assigned sex at birth, which puts trans women at risk of assault. Some shelters have addressed these problems by creating trans-only spaces. At the Salvation Army in Las Vegas, Nevada, these spaces are called safety dorms. The safety dorms provide a sense of acceptance and safety for people who have never felt much of either. They also provide a much-needed refuge for trans people experiencing homelessness, according to resident Shannon Melissa. She adds, "While we have nothing, we are being treated with some dignity and respect. There's always a second chance."[18]

Some end up living outside their preferred locations. Others are forced to pay more than what they can afford. Many end up without any place to stay at all. Thirty percent of trans people have been homeless at some point in their lives.[19] Long-term homelessness can negatively impact a person's career opportunities.

This can decrease their income and lessen their chances of finding stable, affordable housing. It is a vicious cycle that's hard to break.

Some colleges and universities are trying to prevent the cycle from even starting. According to Campus Pride, a nonprofit organization focused on creating safe living and learning environments for LGBTQ college students, more than 250 colleges and universities in the United States offer gender-inclusive housing.[20] That means there are facilities on campus where students can room with anyone of any gender.

WALKING WHILE TRANS

Many law enforcement officers incorrectly assume that all transgender women engage in sex work, which is illegal in most places. Being singled out for one's gender identity by police is sometimes called "walking while trans." And it can be very dangerous. According to the 2015 USTS, 8 percent of all trans people had been harassed by police officers within the previous year because of their gender identity. Of those who perform sex work, 27 percent of respondents reported instances of sexual assault by police officers. Eighteen percent have been physically assaulted. Many crimes against trans people go unreported. The victims often don't feel safe with law enforcement.[21]

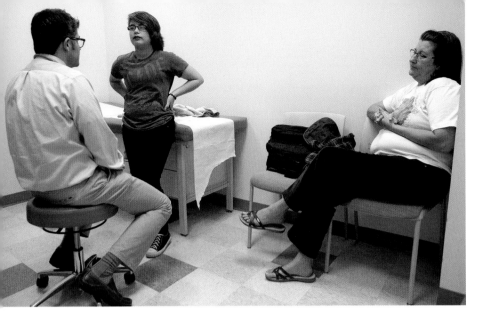

Trans people may see a variety of doctors and mental health professionals while they transition.

That's very helpful for trans students who may not feel comfortable in a single-gender dorm or who don't define themselves with a binary label.

HEALTH CARE

Lucy, a nonbinary trans woman, was required to see a mental health professional before she could start HRT. She began seeing a trans therapist who provided what Lucy felt like was gender-affirming care. According to Lucy, her experience with her therapist has been "surprisingly positive."[22] And Samuel Horton-Martin, a trans man interviewed by *National Geographic*, stated that his primary doctor provided incredible care. He added, "She's aware, she's respectful—she respects my gender identity and my pronouns—and she understands the complexities of treating trans patients."[23]

When trans people do not receive gender-affirming care, it can put their health at risk. According to the 2015 USTS, 33 percent of trans people have had "at least one negative interaction" with health-care professionals in the past year. This includes verbal harassment and refusal of treatment. It also includes instances in which trans people had to educate their health-care provider about being transgender in order to receive proper medical care. Nearly 25 percent of trans people chose not to seek help for a medical condition because they feared they would be mistreated or misunderstood.[24]

Cost is also a factor in a person's choice to seek health care. Gender-affirming surgical procedures can be incredibly expensive, ranging anywhere from $12,000 to $50,000 depending on the procedure. HRT can cost anywhere from $300 to $2,400 per year.[25] These major expenses put the trans community at an economic disadvantage when they are already earning less than their cisgender peers on average.

DISCUSSION STARTERS

- Think of a time when you had a negative experience at school. How did it make you feel? How did you feel about school afterward?

- Should the government have a say in defining gender? Why or why not?

- How can health-care discrimination affect a person's quality of life?

Supportive friends, family, and romantic partners make transitioning less stressful.

HEALTH AND
SAFETY CHALLENGES

Scientific studies and education have gone a long way to decrease the stigma once associated with nonheterosexual people and their relationships. However, this education hasn't fully included information on noncisgender people. Part of the problem is a societal "belief that there is something morally wrong with being transgender," says Harper Jean Tobin, the director of policy at the NCTE.[1] Though trans people are more visible than ever before, a lot of misinformation exists. Many people in the United States view gender identity as a moral choice, not a biological determination. According to Tobin, that belief creates discrimination and violence against trans people.

HARASSMENT AND VIOLENCE

Cisgender people show bias against trans people in a variety of ways. The severity ranges from microaggressions, such as joking about someone's appearance or mocking their decision

to transition, to blatant acts of discrimination. In some cases, prejudice and hate lead to acts of violence. According to the 2015 USTS, 46 percent of transgender people were verbally harassed in the previous year because of their gender identity. Nine percent were victims of physical attacks, such as being punched, having something thrown at them, or being assaulted with a weapon. More than half of all survey respondents experienced some sort of physical, emotional, or financial harm at the hands of romantic partners.[2]

THE DANGERS OF CONVERSION THERAPY

There are several groups, most of them affiliated with fundamentalist religious communities, that claim being anything other than cisgender and straight is abnormal. They also claim they can "fix" people through a process known as conversion therapy.

Conversion therapy takes many forms. It can range from conversations about one's feelings to hypnosis or even physical abuse. Every leading professional medical and mental health association has spoken out against conversion therapy. It is not only ineffective but also incredibly harmful. Conversion therapy is known to cause feelings of depression, guilt, shame, hopelessness, and self-hatred in its subjects. This can lead to loss of friends, loss of faith, withdrawal from society, substance abuse, and even suicide.

As of February 2019, 15 states and Washington, DC, had passed laws preventing licensed mental health professionals from administering conversion therapy to minors. However, these laws did not prohibit people from practicing unlicensed conversion therapy. They also did not penalize the adults who force minors into conversion therapy.

Just under 50 percent of survey respondents said they had been sexually assaulted at some point in their lives. Ten percent were sexually assaulted in the year prior to the survey. An anonymous survey respondent who shared their experiences said groping and verbal harassment occur because "[people] can't figure out whether I am a 'man' or a 'woman' and they think they have the right to demand an explanation."[3]

According to trans advocates, violence against trans people is only getting worse. Some believe this is related to the cultural and political changes that accompanied Donald Trump's presidential election. "There is an increased climate of hate that is, in some cases, being allowed to grow," said Beverly Tillery, executive director of the New York City Anti-Violence Project.[4] The rising murder rate also shows an increase in hostility toward the trans community. Twenty-one trans people were murdered in 2015. This rose to 23 people in 2016. There were 26 transgender murder victims in 2017, plus another 16 in the first eight months of 2018.[5]

EFFECTS ON PHYSICAL HEALTH

Discrimination aimed at the transgender community can damage its members' physical and mental well-being. A study published in the *Journal of the American Medical Association* in 2017 indicates people who are transgender are more likely to be in overall poorer health than their cisgender peers. The study

Trans children protested in February 2017 when the Trump administration removed protections for trans students in public schools.

was based on results of a survey administered by the US Centers for Disease Control and Prevention (CDC). It showed that transgender people are more likely to be overweight than cisgender people (72 percent versus 66 percent). They are also less likely to have health insurance (79 percent versus 89 percent).[6]

Many experts attribute the heightened health risks to stress. Stress produces a hormone called cortisol. High cortisol levels contribute to many medical problems, including high blood pressure, weight gain, decreased learning and memory, increased likelihood of heart disease, and a weak immune system. Consistently high cortisol levels can eventually lead to a decline in brainpower. It can also lead to increased risk of Alzheimer's disease, a brain disorder that includes memory loss.

HARDSHIPS FOR TRANS PEOPLE OF COLOR

Violence against members of the transgender community is disproportionately focused on trans women of color (TWOC). Experts at the Human Rights Campaign (HRC) believe this is because TWOC are at the "intersections of racism, sexism, homophobia and transphobia."[7] In general, trans people of color experience higher rates of poverty, unemployment, and assault than cisgender people of color and white transgender people. Though their "double-minority" status doesn't double the rate of discrimination, it does make personal safety and societal acceptance harder to achieve. However, the intersections of identity are nuanced and specific to a person's life situation. Other factors such as class and age also play a part.

EFFECTS ON MENTAL HEALTH

Transgender people are also at a higher risk for stress-induced mental illness. This is partly because of elevated cortisol levels. It is also because of the sense of otherness many transgender people feel in a society that often denies their existence. According to the authors of a 2016 study published in the *Journal of the International AIDS Society*, "Extreme social exclusion and lack of acceptance of transgender populations . . . diminishes [a transgender person's] self-esteem and ability to participate in social events."[10] This can lead to ongoing distress, depression, and anxiety.

The results of the 2017 *Journal of the American Medical Association* study indicate that 22 percent of trans adults have been diagnosed with depression. That's approximately

Mental health support may include individual or group therapy.

4 percent higher than the rate of diagnosed depression in cis respondents from the same survey.[11] Perhaps even more alarming is the staggeringly high risk for suicide in the transgender community. According to the 2015 USTS, nearly 82 percent of trans people have had suicidal thoughts at least once in their lifetimes.[12]

Support from family, friends, and health-care professionals can be a stabilizing force during times of anxiety and distress. "I struggled a lot for many years because of how my body looked after puberty," a trans person named Chris wrote in a 2015 editorial for the *New York Times*. The unwavering support Chris received from their therapist, girlfriend, and good friends was instrumental in getting Chris through such a difficult time. "I survived and am living a much better life now," Chris wrote.[13]

CHALLENGES OF RECOVERY

Getting help for alcohol and substance abuse can be difficult for transgender people, particularly if they require 24-hour rehabilitative care. Many rehab centers segregate patients by gender. This can cause further feelings of otherness if the facility determines gender by birth assignment, not gender identity. Some rehab centers may not be equipped to maintain a trans patient's HRT regimen. Caretakers within the facility may not understand the psychological importance of HRT in a patient's recovery. These same issues, as well as concerns about personal safety, also affect transgender people in jails and prisons.

When trans people cannot find adequate mental health care, they may turn to risky coping methods such as substance use. Nearly 30 percent of respondents on the 2015 USTS reported using illicit drugs, marijuana, or recreational prescription drugs in the previous month.[14] Ongoing feelings of shame lead to low self-esteem and depression, which some people deal with in dangerous ways. Kris T. De Pedro, the lead author of a 2017 study about transgender teens and drug use, told NBC News that drug-abuse prevention programs aren't enough to prevent trans people, especially teens, from engaging in risky behaviors. "We really need to fill a fundamental need for [transgender] kids, and that's the need to feel accepted and affirmed," he said.[15]

DISCUSSION STARTERS

- Do you think there is a connection between mental health and physical health? Provide examples to support your theories.

- Why is it unsafe for trans people to avoid medical care? What can be done to change how often trans people seek medical care?

- Why is it important to have a support system?

TRANS PEOPLE
IN THE MEDIA

H ate and intolerance are learned behaviors. Just like no one is born disliking people because of the color of their skin, there are no genetic triggers for disliking a person because of their gender identity. Instead, negative beliefs and feelings develop over time. They are influenced by a variety of sources, such as the media one consumes, family values, teachings of faith, and personal experiences.

MEDIA MATTERS

The things a person reads, sees, or hears shape the way they view the world. For example, someone who only reads articles about how great year-round schooling is will probably support their school district's decision to switch to that schedule. Someone who only hears negative things about it would not support that decision.

THE FIRST TRANS CELEBRITY

In 1950, Christine Jorgensen sailed to Europe from the United States. She was in search of medical professionals who could help her transform her body into one that matched her gender identity. Two years, two surgeries, and "massive doses" of estrogen later, the former soldier was on the front page of the *New York Daily News*. The headline read, "Ex-GI Becomes Blonde Beauty: Operations Transform Bronx Youth."[1] When the glamorous Jorgensen returned to the United States in January 1953, she was already a celebrity.

Jorgensen was one of the first trans people to find themselves under the watchful eye of the mass media. Reporters' descriptions about her varied from fawning to cruel. More than one insisted she was nothing more than a man with severe psychological problems. But Jorgensen's story also spurred a flurry of scientific research about gender and sexuality. Perhaps most importantly, it introduced cisgender people in the United States to the concept of gender-affirming surgery and gave hope to those who had been struggling in the shadows.

That's how it works with transgender representation in the media. Trans characters in television shows and movies are often portrayed as being mentally disturbed outcasts or sexual deviants. Those stereotypes stick with the audience and affect their own attitudes about members of the trans community. The same thing occurs in the news media. Stories that focus on a subject's otherness reinforce the idea that trans people do not belong in mainstream society.

Positive depictions of transgender people in the media have the power to educate and enlighten people who have no idea what it is like to be trans. They can also be a lifeline for people struggling with feelings of isolation and despair due to their own gender identity. Some trans advocates even think that increased visibility in the media may decrease the trans suicide rate.

Those are some of the reasons journalist and author Janet Mock disclosed her trans identity in a 2011 issue of *Marie Claire* magazine. When she was growing up in Hawaii and California, positive stories about trans people were few and far between. "I'd never seen a young trans woman who was living and thriving in the world, and I was looking for that," Mock said in a 2018 interview with the *Guardian*. According to Mock, trans people "don't just need to know the tragedy and trauma of being trans. They also need to know how to better be, how to better live, how to better dream."[2] Positive media representation helps with that.

INCREASING VISIBILITY

Until very recently, trans peoples' stories were hard to find in popular culture. A few trans characters, often played by cis actors, would pop up as minor characters on criminal procedural television shows such as *CSI* and *Law & Order*. A handful of movies, such as *Boys Don't Cry* (1999) and *Transamerica* (2005), provided more in-depth looks at trans characters. However, these roles were also played by cis actors.

Prior to the 2010s, most representations of trans people on-screen fed into negative stereotypes. In 2012, the

LGBTQ-focused media advocacy group GLAAD discovered that 40 percent of trans characters on prime-time television shows between 2002 and 2012 were depicted as victims. More than 20 percent were portrayed as killers or villains, and 20 percent were cast as sex workers.[3] In addition to reinforcing stereotypes, these roles were small and rarely extended beyond one episode. Viewers never saw a trans character develop over the course of an entire season. Trans actors trying to get into television had little chance of securing ongoing employment.

Things began to change in 2007. ABC's new prime-time drama *Dirty Sexy Money* featured a trans character who was also a love interest of one of the cisgender main characters. Carmelita was played by Candis Cayne, the first openly trans actor to have a recurring role on a prime-time network television show.

DROP IN THE BUCKET

In mid-2017, GLAAD counted only 17 trans characters out of 901 recurring characters on broadcast scripted prime-time television. The 17 includes characters on *Mr. Robot*, *The Fosters*, *The OA*, *Star*, and *Transparent*. New shows such as *Pose* increased those numbers in 2018, but they still made up just a small fraction of the stories told on television. Most of the shows featuring realistic portrayals of trans characters are on cable networks or streaming services like Netflix and Amazon, all of which require fee-based subscriptions. Cable subscriptions also require annual fees. This leaves out a large segment of the population that does not purchase these services.

On *Orange Is the New Black*, Laverne Cox's character, Sophia, *right*, discusses her gender identity with her son.

In 2008, Isis King became the first trans contestant on *America's Next Top Model*, and in 2009, reality show *The Real World* cast its first trans housemate, Katelynn Cusanelli.

For many trans advocates and pop culture enthusiasts, trans people officially became part of mainstream culture in 2013 when Netflix debuted *Orange Is the New Black*. Based on the memoir of the same name, the show explores the lives and relationships of fictional characters serving time in a women's prison. Sophia, a trans woman hairdresser, soon became a fan favorite. So did Laverne Cox, the trans actor who plays her. "People are not just feeling for Sophia, who is a black trans woman, they are feeling for the actor Laverne who is also a black trans woman," Cox said in a 2017 interview with the *Telegraph.* "That's really what we need more of. To feel empathy for a person who's in a different circumstance than we're in."[4]

Cox quickly became one of the most visible transgender women in the world. In 2014, she became the first trans person to appear on the cover of *Time* magazine and was named to the magazine's list of 100 most influential people. Cox didn't use her time in the spotlight just to talk about her career. She dispelled myths about the trans community, educated audiences about the realities of being trans, and emphasized the importance of listening to trans voices.

In April 2014, 65-year-old Olympic gold medalist and reality television star Caitlyn Jenner came out as a transgender woman. Caitlyn shared her story in a televised interview with Diane Sawyer on ABC's *20/20* and in an article in *Vanity Fair.* Some trans advocates and media critics consider Jenner's coming out to be a landmark moment in the trans community. This type of public representation not only helps alleviate the stigma associated with being transgender but also lets people exploring their own gender identity know they are not alone.

TWO STEPS FORWARD, ONE STEP BACK

Trans people are more visible in media than ever before. In 2018, trans actor Nicole Maines became television's first trans superhero on *Supergirl*. That same year, *Pose* premiered. *Pose* is a drama about drag ball culture set in the 1980s. It has the largest cast of transgender actors in major roles and the greatest number of recurring LGBTQ cast members.

However, there is still an enormous amount of work to be done in both entertainment and news media. One of the biggest criticisms of trans characters in movies and television is that they are often

PRIVILEGED AND TRANS

Some trans advocates have questioned whether Caitlyn Jenner is the best representation of the trans community. As a wealthy, privileged white woman, she experiences little of the economic and social discrimination of her trans peers. She voted for Donald Trump, who during his presidency has rolled back many of the trans-friendly policies enacted by Barack Obama's administration. After Trump's administration ended federal protections allowing students to use the bathroom that aligned with their gender identity, Jenner tweeted to the president, "From one Republican to another, this is a disaster. You made a promise to protect the LGBTQ community. Call me."[5]

Jenner doesn't regret her vote, but she is deeply disappointed in Trump's policies. In a 2018 interview with *Variety*, Jenner stated that she was lobbying for trans rights with legislators in Washington, DC. According to Jenner, Trump "[has] not been doing a very good job, but it's not over yet."[6]

The FX show *Pose* features many trans actors, such as Indya Moore, *pictured*, who plays Angel Evangelista.

played by cisgender actors. For example, Jeffrey Tambor starred in the first four seasons of *Transparent*, which was initially about a family dealing with its patriarch's transition to womanhood. Jared Leto won an Academy Award for his role as a trans woman in 2013's *Dallas Buyers Club*. In 2015, Eddie Redmayne played Lili Elbe, one of the first people to undergo gender-affirming surgery, in *The Danish Girl*.

These cisgender men earned critical acclaim for their portrayals. But many people believe trans actors should be first in line for playing trans characters. Trans actor and writer Jen Richards said in a 2018 interview, "The issue is that trans people often can't get in the door. . . . We're not even considered for parts that *aren't* trans, so when we can't even get in the door for trans roles it just leaves us in a completely untenable situation."[7] Nonbinary actor Ellie Desautels echoed Richards in an interview with *Teen Vogue*, saying:

TRANS REPRESENTATION IN VIDEO GAMES

The few transgender video game characters that do exist aren't always portrayed in the most positive light. A 2016 study by Adrienne Shaw and Elizaveta Friesem noted that often with trans characters, their "gender is treated as a problem to be dealt with by other characters."[8] In other cases, characters may be coded, or perceived, as trans, though their gender identity is not stated.

One major exception to that is Krem from *Dragon Age: Inquisition* (2014). Though he is not a playable character, he has a full backstory that gives details about his gender identity. To make sure they got it right, the game's cisgender writer and editors sent the game's script to a few genderqueer friends. The friends revised several areas that were either offensive or played into typical trans stereotypes.

> I've heard other stories from trans women and trans-feminine people about their not-so-good experiences. Many of them weren't considered for transgender roles because they

Ellie Desautels, who is nonbinary, played the trans character Michael Hallowell on the NBC show *Rise*.

"don't look trans enough." That idea, that trans characters need to look a certain way, rules out many trans artists. It also devalues us as people by saying trans people must "look trans."[9]

Some people in Hollywood are starting to listen. In 2018, Scarlett Johansson was set to play Dante "Tex" Gill, a 1970s Pittsburgh crime boss who was also a trans man, in a movie. People were upset that the role was being played by a cis woman. After weeks of controversy, Johansson withdrew herself from the project. As of December 2018, it was unknown whether the movie would be made, as it was Johansson's name that had attracted financing.

Big names like Johansson's attract viewers. Television and movie studios are often hesitant to risk money on projects that don't have a guarantee of success. Because there are so few opportunities for trans people in the media, there are few trans

REPRESENTATION BEHIND THE SCENES

Several transgender writers, producers, and directors are working hard to make sure trans stories are heard, seen, and read. Jill Soloway, who identifies as nonbinary, is the creator, writer, and director of *Transparent*, which is based on their own parent's late-in-life transition. Journalist, author, and advocate Janet Mock is a writer and producer of *Pose*. Artist Sophie Campbell introduced a transgender character, Blaze, to comic *Jem and the Holograms* and helped cowrite Blaze's coming-out story for issue 12.

Jenna Talackova made it to the finals of the Miss Universe Canada pageant.

people with enough "star power" to convince studio executives they'll get a return on their investment.

There's also room for improvement in how the news media tells trans stories. In 2012, Miss Universe Canada contestant Jenna Talackova attracted attention for her dismissal from and reinstatement to the pageant. She is a trans woman.

Reporters scrambled to interview Talackova. But instead of talking about the beauty contest, many interviewers focused on Talackova's body and personal life. "So if I saw you undressed, you would look like a woman to me totally, yes?" asked Barbara Walters.[10] Canadian newspaper the *Vancouver Sun* ran a story about Talackova with the headline "Transgender Beauty Queen Jenna Talackova Has a Boyfriend, Hopes to Have Children."[11] Questions and stories like these dehumanize transgender people. They reinforce the negative stereotypes of them being freaks and outsiders. Journalists have a professional obligation to report about their subjects fairly and without bias. Like entertainment media, news outlets shape the way people see the world and, in many cases, themselves.

DISCUSSION STARTERS

- Think about the media you consume. What media and topics affect how you feel about yourself? Which things do you pay attention to, and which do you ignore? Why?

- Many trans advocates say only trans actors should play trans characters. Do you agree with this? Why or why not?

- Who, if any, are the trans characters in the media you consume? Are you able to relate to them? Why or why not?

THE TRANS YOUTUBE GENERATION

Today, the internet is often the first stop for people who are questioning their gender identity or sexuality. At one point or another, most people end up on YouTube, which has become the unofficial home for young transgender and gender-nonconforming people looking for and sharing information. "I can't tell you how many hours I spent scrolling through story after story of those who had transitioned or were transitioning before me," wrote Arin Andrews in his 2014 memoir *Some Assembly Required*. Andrews was especially drawn to the videos of Skylar Kergil, also known as Skylarkeleven. "He gave me the answers and hope I was searching for," Andrews wrote.[12]

Kergil and other trans YouTubers, including Chase Ross, Gigi Loren Lazzarato, Stef Sanjati, and Miles McKenna, share some of the most intimate parts of their lives with their viewers. Their unspoken purpose is twofold. The first is to reach out to viewers who are either questioning their own gender identity or looking for a community that will support them. Trans YouTubers describe what it is like to transition, answer questions, and share their hopes and fears about their own lives.

The other purpose is to decrease the stigma associated with being transgender. Many popular trans YouTubers share videos of themselves doing everyday things, such as shopping, playing music, and goofing around in front of the camera. These types of videos assure viewers, particularly those who are cisgender, that trans people aren't any different from anyone else.

In 2018, YouTuber Miles McKenna won the award for Best LGBTQ+ Account at the Shorty Awards.

8

THE FUTURE OF TRANSGENDER EQUALITY

T he experience of being transgender in the United States has changed dramatically since the early 1900s. Advancements in psychological and medical research have helped ease some of the stigma attached to the transgender community. Trans advocates and allies have worked hard to move past the negative portrayals of transgender people in popular culture while championing the rights of the trans community.

These efforts have led to a trans population that is more visible. More and more people are taking the risk of publicly identifying as trans. By taking charge of their gender identities, they're also taking steps to ensure their future health and happiness.

Many LGBTQ people of faith have trouble reconciling who they are with the teachings of their religion. For example, the Roman Catholic Church believes that gender is permanently decided at birth. It does not recognize gender transition. The Church of Jesus Christ of Latter-day Saints will not baptize or confirm people who are considering "elective transsexual operations."[1] Many evangelical churches refuse to accept transgender members at all.

This denial of a person's sense of self causes many members of the LGBTQ community to distance themselves from religion. A 2013 survey by the Pew Research Center indicated 48 percent of LGBTQ adults had no religious affiliation. In the general population, that number is only 20 percent. One-third of LGBTQ adults also said there was "a conflict between their religious beliefs and their sexual orientation or gender identity."[2]

However, as understanding of sexual orientation and gender identity increases, so does religious acceptance. The Episcopal Church, Reform Judaism, the Unitarian Universalist Association, and the United Church of Christ have all said they accept people of all gender identities. The Evangelical Lutheran Church of America, the Presbyterian Church, and the United Methodist Church also welcome trans people.

Social and political progress is never easy. There's still a lot of work to be done to ensure gender identity equality in the United States. Some of that work needs to take place at the levels of federal and state government. Some belongs to private organizations and institutions. But the biggest changes will come from people standing up for trans rights.

WHERE WE ARE

In many parts of US life, members of the transgender community are still treated like second-class citizens. President Trump has issued executive orders that roll back protections for trans people. Transgender and gender-nonconforming Americans can be fired from their jobs, denied medical care, and evicted from their homes because of their gender identity. As of January 2019, they can no longer enlist in the military, and they aren't protected from bullying or other forms of harassment such as verbal abuse in a public restroom.

However, there are some bright spots. More than a dozen individual states have adopted their own laws prohibiting discrimination based on a person's gender identity. The EEOC, which enforces employment law in the United States, publicly stated in 2016 that transgender and gender-nonconforming people are protected from discrimination in the workplace by Title VII of the Civil Rights Act of 1964.

The Affordable Care Act, passed in 2010, prohibits insurance companies that receive federal funding or offer plans on the government marketplace from discriminating against

TRANS MUSICIANS TO WATCH

In 2012, Laura Jane Grace of the punk band Against Me! came out as a trans woman. In 2014, the band released the critically acclaimed album *Transgender Dysphoria Blues*, which Grace wrote during her transition. Other trans and genderfluid artists making waves in the music industry include Oscar-nominated Anohni, two-spirit pop singer and songwriter She King (also known as Shawnee Talbot), indie punk rocker Mal Blum, indie pop singer A.W., and rapper KC Ortiz.

transgender people. That means they can't deny someone coverage because they are trans. They also cannot refuse to pay for transition-related care. It also prohibits discrimination by health-care programs, providers, and organizations that receive federal funding, including Medicare and Medicaid.

Individual employers are also paying more attention to their trans employees than ever before. According to the HRC's 2017 Corporate Equality Index, 82 percent of Fortune 500 companies have antidiscrimination policies that explicitly prohibit harassment or bias based on gender identity.[3] One-half of these companies also offer health-care plans that cover transition-related care.

Transgender people and their stories are more visible in the media than ever before. Instead of being relegated to stereotypical victim or villain roles, increasing numbers of trans characters on television and in movies are portrayed as having full, interesting lives that have little to

MORE THAN COMING OUT

Trans people are more than just their coming-out stories. That's why some media critics are pushing for the inclusion of trans characters in stories that have nothing to do with gender identity. Comics such as *The Backstagers*, *Batgirl*, *The Wicked + The Divine*, *Jem and the Holograms*, and *Lumberjanes* are already doing this by including characters who just happen to be trans. So is the animated television show *Steven Universe*, which takes place in a world where nonbinary genders are the norm.

do with their gender identity. Trans actors are using their newfound visibility to educate the public, which helps dispel trans myths and builds empathetic connections.

THE ONGOING BATTLE FOR EQUALITY

One of the first steps to ensuring equal and fair treatment for members of the trans community is creating or amending federal legislation. Organizations such as Lambda Legal and the American Civil Liberties Union tackle this head-on through lawsuits and petitions for changes to public policy. One of the major goals of groups like these is to amend the Civil Rights Act of 1964 to explicitly prohibit discrimination and denial of services based on a person's gender identity. This will alleviate any confusion about what is and what isn't allowed in schools, hospitals, places of employment, real estate transactions, and public facilities.

States and local municipalities are also shaping laws to be more inclusive of trans students. In May 2018, New Hampshire became the first state since 2016 to prohibit gender identity discrimination in employment, housing, and public spaces. State representatives from both sides of the aisle came together to support the measure. More than 200 cities around the country have their own legislation guaranteeing civil rights

With more inclusive employment protections, trans people can feel safe expressing their gender identity at work.

for trans people.[4] This is particularly important for cities in states that do not have statewide legislation prohibiting discrimination based on gender identity.

Individual people are working toward civil rights too. Many trans members of the US military have spoken out against President Trump's ban on new transgender service members. "'Divide and conquer' is not something that should happen within [the military]; the military needs to stay united in order to stay strong," said Emery van Broekhuizen of the US Army Reserve in a 2018 *Time* magazine article. Jayceon Taylor of the US Army agrees. "How I define myself should not ban me from serving my country," he said in the same article.[5]

Large and small organizations alike are tackling issues with trans health care. Lambda Legal and other advocacy organizations continue to represent those who have been denied access to transition-related health care. Smaller groups—such as Transgender Healthcare Group, which is based in Madison, Wisconsin—connect trans patients with trans-friendly health-care providers and insurance. Since 2007, the HRC has rated local and regional health-care facilities in its annual "Healthcare Equality Index." This free, online document highlights medical facilities that provide respectful and comprehensive care for LGBTQ patients.

LEADING BY EXAMPLE

Bias and discrimination often come from a misunderstanding of what it means to be trans. That's why one of the most important components of trans equality is education of the cisgender population. Many institutions, such as businesses, hospitals, and schools, are stepping up to take responsibility for the health and safety of their trans employees, patients, clients, and students.

Hundreds of schools across the United States allow trans students access to restrooms and locker rooms of their choice. Many also allow trans students to participate in gender-based, school-sponsored activities that match their gender identities. This may include athletic teams, dance and cheer teams,

Some schools have switched to gender-neutral restrooms in order to accommodate the needs of trans students.

and choirs. More than 6,500 schools around the United States support gay-straight alliances or gender-sexuality alliances, also known as GSAs.[6] These are student-led clubs that help foster feelings of safety and inclusion for LGBTQ students and their allies. The LGBTQ school advocacy group GLSEN has several resources for students who want to start GSAs at their schools.

Some employers are taking steps not only to ensure job safety for their trans employees but also to make sure they are treated respectfully by customers and clients. For example, two restaurants in Minneapolis, Minnesota, have placed signs near the registers that ask customers to use gender-neutral language when addressing employees. The owners and staff members at May Day Cafe and Taco Cat believe this simple shift in language creates a safe space for trans and genderqueer employees.

They also want to start a larger conversation about inclusion and acceptance.

Activism and education is also on the rise in the medical community. One of the leaders of this movement is Jack Turban. He is a medical writer and child and adolescent psychiatrist at Harvard Medical School. His focus is pediatric gender identity and how health-care providers can best serve trans children. With his guidance, the Yale School of Medicine and other medical schools have developed a curriculum. It is specifically designed to teach medical students how to care for trans patients. "My hope is that we will create a new generation of compassionate, informed physicians who can help these patients thrive," Turban told *Bustle* in 2017.[7] He and other medical professionals are also fighting against the rampant spread of misinformation about the trans population within the medical community.

Media also plays an important role in educating the public

THE FUTURE OF THE FASHION INDUSTRY

Model Rain Dove is breaking the mold in an industry that has only just begun to include transgender models in its runway shows and advertising campaigns. The nonbinary Dove, who refers to themself as a "gender capitalist," presents as either male or female depending on the job. "I can basically go to any casting I want to as long as somebody likes my face," they said in an interview with *Bustle* magazine.[8] Dove is also highly active on social media, where they share thoughts and experiments about gender expression and nonconformity.

about gender identity and the trans community. GLAAD's Media Reference Guide is available on its website. Many news media organizations, such as newspapers, magazines, news broadcasts, and news websites, follow the standards set forth in this guide. It educates people about terminology, pronoun usage, and defamatory language. Fictional depictions of trans people in media such as television, movies, comic books, novels, and computer games are starting to move away from negative stereotypes of trans and genderqueer characters. This is in part because of trans-inclusive hiring practices. These practices put trans writers, editors, actors, and production team members in charge of telling trans stories.

Progress for transgender rights often comes after activists and organizations speak out against injustice.

Economic, political, and social barriers still stand in the way of trans equality and acceptance. Activist groups are working to change minds and laws so all people can feel safe and accepted. That work is helped by the trans people who bravely share their own stories in the hope of ending the stigma and stereotypes associated with their community. Though progress can seem painstakingly slow, every small step forward in equality and acceptance makes an enormous impact on the lives of the next trans generation.

DISCUSSION STARTERS

- Which do you think would be more effective at protecting transgender people's rights: laws at the state level or laws at the national level? Why?

- What types of educational materials, either formal or informal, have helped you develop opinions about the transgender community? How did you access those materials?

- How can cisgender people be allies to transgender friends and family? Provide examples.

ESSENTIAL FACTS

SIGNIFICANT EVENTS

- In 2007, Jazz Jennings and her family were interviewed by Barbara Walters. This interview helped propel trans children and their struggles into the national spotlight.

- In 2013, the *Diagnostic and Statistical Manual of Mental Disorders* (*DSM*) was updated to include gender dysphoria, the psychological stress caused by having a gender that does not align with the sex a person was assigned at birth. Gender identity disorder was also removed from this version of the DSM. Previously, a diagnosis of gender identity disorder meant that a trans person needed to be "cured" of their gender identity.

- In 2017, President Donald Trump issued a ban on transgender people serving in the military. This reversed a 2016 decision by President Barack Obama. In January 2019, the Supreme Court ruled that the ban could remain in place while court cases about the ban made their way through the federal courts.

KEY PLAYERS

- Caitlyn Jenner is a reality television star and Olympic medalist. She is a prominent transgender celebrity and is also a member of the Republican Party.

- Laverne Cox is an actress and activist who stars on the show *Orange Is the New Black*. She was one of the first trans people to have a continuing role in a television series.

IMPACT ON SOCIETY

Transgender people are often denied basic civil rights. Discrimination based on gender identity extends into education, health care, employment, housing, military service, and even public restrooms. Because of this, transgender people often make less money than their cisgender peers, which can push some into unsafe living and working conditions. This will continue until federal and state laws explicitly include protections for gender identity in antidiscrimination legislation.

QUOTE

"We really need to fill a fundamental need for [transgender] kids, and that's the need to feel accepted and affirmed."

—Kris T. De Pedro, lead author of a 2017 study about transgender teens and drug use

GLOSSARY

ADVOCATE
A person who actively supports a cause, policy, or group.

ALLY
A person or group who gives help to another person or group.

ANDROGYNOUS
Having both male and female characteristics or qualities.

CISGENDER (CIS)
Having a gender identity that matches the sex they were assigned at birth.

DEFAMATORY
Meant to hurt the reputation of someone or something.

DISHONORABLE DISCHARGE
The ending of a person's military service because of unacceptable behavior.

FORTUNE 500
An annual list, published by *Fortune* magazine, of the 500 companies in the United States with the highest revenue that year.

GENDER DYSPHORIA
The distress caused by having a gender identity that does not match the sex assigned at birth.

GENDER EXPRESSION
The outward appearance of someone's gender identity.

GENDER IDENTITY
A person's perception of their gender, which may or may not correspond with the sex they were assigned at birth.

PATHOLOGIZE
To regard or treat someone as psychologically abnormal or unhealthy.

PUBERTY
The beginning of physical maturity when a person becomes capable of reproducing sexually.

SECONDARY SEX CHARACTERISTIC
A physical characteristic that appears in members of one sex at puberty but is not directly related to reproduction. Breasts, facial hair, pubic hair, and deepening voices are all secondary sex characteristics.

SEX WORK
The exchange of money or goods for sexual services.

SEXUALLY DIMORPHIC
Relating to characteristics that are different between the sexes of the same species.

STIGMA
A set of negative and often unfair beliefs that a society or group of people has about something.

TRANSGENDER (TRANS)
Having a gender identity that does not match the sex they were assigned at birth.

URETHRA
The tube through which urine moves from the bladder and out of the body.

ADDITIONAL RESOURCES

SELECTED BIBLIOGRAPHY

"The Report of the 2015 US Transgender Survey." *National Center for Transgender Equality*, Dec. 2016, transequality.org. Accessed 17 Jan. 2019.

"Military Service by Transgender Individuals." *Presidential Memorandum for the Secretary of Defense and the Secretary of Homeland Security*, US Government, 25 Aug. 2017, whitehouse.gov. Accessed 17 Jan. 2019.

"What Is Gender Dysphoria?" *American Psychiatric Association*, 2018, psychiatry.org. Accessed 26 Nov. 2018.

FURTHER READINGS

Andrews, Arin. *Some Assembly Required: The Not-So-Secret Life of a Transgender Teen*. Simon, 2014.

Harris, Duchess, and Martha Lundin. *LGBTQ Rights and the Law*. Abdo, 2020.

Jennings, Jazz. *Being Jazz: My Life as a (Transgender) Teen*. Crown, 2016.

ONLINE RESOURCES

To learn more about being transgender in America, please visit **abdobooklinks.com** or scan this QR code. These links are routinely monitored and updated to provide the most current information available.

MORE INFORMATION

For more information on this subject, contact or visit the following organizations:

HUMAN RIGHTS CAMPAIGN
1640 Rhode Island Ave. NW
Washington, DC 20036-3278
hrc.org

The Human Rights Campaign (HRC) is the largest LGBTQ civil rights organization in the United States. Its mission is to inspire and engage individuals and communities to end LGBTQ discrimination through personal and group action.

MOVEMENT ADVANCEMENT PROJECT
3020 Carbon Pl., Suite 202
Boulder, CO 80301
lgbtmap.org

The Movement Advancement Project (MAP) is an independent organization focused on achieving equal rights for the LGBTQ population. Its website offers research and insight about many issues facing different subsections of the LGBTQ community.

NATIONAL CENTER FOR TRANSGENDER EQUALITY
1133 Nineteenth St. NW, Suite 203
Washington, DC 20036
transequality.org

The National Center for Transgender Equality (NCTE) is dedicated to achieving social justice and equality for transgender people.

SOURCE NOTES

CHAPTER 1. INTRODUCING JAZZ

1. TLC. "All About Jazz." *I Am Jazz*, 15 July 2015, tlc.com. Accessed 17 Jan. 2019.

2. TLC, "All About Jazz."

3. "Transgender at 11: Listening to Jazz Jennings." *YouTube*, uploaded by ABC News, 19 Jan. 2013, youtube.com. Accessed 17 Jan. 2019.

4. Jazz Jennings. *Being Jazz: My Life as a (Transgender) Teen*. Crown, 2016. 7.

5. TLC, "All About Jazz."

6. Jennings, *Being Jazz*, 28–29.

7. Jennings, *Being Jazz*, 46.

8. Lindsey Tanner. "More U.S. Teens Identify as Transgender, Survey Finds." *USA Today*, 5 Feb. 2018, usatoday.com. Accessed 17 Jan. 2019.

9. Noel Alumit. "UCLA Study Finds an Estimated 150,000 US Youths Ages 13–17 Identify as Transgender." *UCLA Newsroom*, 18 Jan. 2017, newsroom.ucla.edu. Accessed 17 Jan. 2019.

10. Jennings, *Being Jazz*, 54.

11. Jennings, *Being Jazz*, 141.

CHAPTER 2. WHAT DOES IT MEAN TO BE TRANSGENDER?

1. Jan Hoffman. "Estimate of U.S. Transgender Population Doubles to 1.4 Million Adults." *New York Times*, 30 June 2016, nytimes.com. Accessed 17 Jan. 2019.

2. Suzannah Weiss. "9 Things People Get Wrong about Being Non-Binary." *Teen Vogue*, 15 Feb. 2018, teenvogue.com. Accessed 17 Jan. 2019.

3. Katy Steinmetz. "Behind the TIME Cover Story: Beyond 'He' or 'She.'" *Time*, 16 Mar. 2017, time.com. Accessed 17 Jan. 2019.

4. Vera Papisova. "What It Means to Identify as Agender." *Teen Vogue*, 20 Jan. 2016, teenvogue.com. Accessed 17 Jan. 2019.

5. Rebecca Nagle. "The Healing History of Two-Spirit, a Term That Gives LGBTQ Natives a Voice." *Huffington Post*, 30 June 2018, huffingtonpost.com. Accessed 17 Jan. 2019.

6. Shanna Collins. "The Splendor of Gender Non-Conformity in Africa." *Medium*, 9 Oct. 2017, medium.com. Accessed 17 Jan. 2019.

7. Cydney Adams. "The Difference between Sexual Orientation and Gender Identity." *CBS News*, 24 Mar. 2017, cbsnews.com. Accessed 17 Jan. 2019.

8. Hope Hedge Seck. "New Trump Transgender Military Policy Bars Those with Gender Dysphoria." *Military.com*, 11 June 2017, military.com. Accessed 17 Jan. 2019.

9. Samantha Allen. "The Search for the 'Transgender Brain' Is Dangerous—and Dehumanizing." *Daily Beast*, 23 May 2018, dailybeast.com. Accessed 17 Jan. 2019.

CHAPTER 3. EXPRESSING GENDER IDENTITY

1. Ashleigh Buch. "Coming Out: A Transgender Airmen's Story." *Task & Purpose*, 25 Aug. 2018, taskandpurpose.com. Accessed 17 Jan. 2019.

2. Jaclyn M. White Hughto and Sari L. Reisner. "A Systematic Review of the Effects of Hormone Therapy on Psychological Functioning and Quality of Life in Transgender Individuals." *Transgender Health*, 1 Jan. 2016, liebertpub.com. Accessed 17 Jan. 2019.

3. Lane Moore. "What It's Really Like to Transition from Female to Male." *Cosmopolitan*, 15 Jan. 2016, cosmopolitan.com. Accessed 17 Jan. 2019.

4. Crystal Raypoole. "What Does It Mean for a Transgender Person to Transition?" *GoodTherapy*, 29 June 2016, goodtherapy.org. Accessed 17 Jan. 2019.

5. Susan Milligan. "Isolated and Left Behind." *U.S. News & World Report*, 16 July 2018, usnews.com. Accessed 17 Jan. 2019.

CHAPTER 4. LEGAL CHALLENGES

1. Bryan Stevenson. "Meet the 31 People Who Are Changing the South." *Time*, 26 Jul. 2018, time.com. Accessed 17 Jan. 2019.

2. "The Report of the 2015 US Transgender Survey." *National Center for Transgender Equality*, Dec. 2016, transequality.org. Accessed 17 Jan. 2019.

3. GJ Gates and JL Herman. "Transgender Military Service in the United States." *Williams Institute, UCLA School of Law*, May 2014, williamsinstitute.law.ucla.edu. Accessed 17 Jan. 2019.

4. Office for Civil Rights. "Title IX and Sex Discrimination." *US Department of Education*, 25 Sept. 2018, ed.gov. Accessed 17 Jan. 2019.

5. Zeke J. Miller. "President Trump Has Taken a Key Step to Implement His Transgender Military Ban." *Time*, 25 Aug. 2017, time.com. Accessed 17 Jan. 2019.

6. "Military Service by Transgender Individuals." *Presidential Memorandum for the Secretary of Defense and the Secretary of Homeland Security, US Government*, 25 Aug. 2017, whitehouse.gov. Accessed 17 Jan. 2019.

7. Movement Advancement Project. "Name Change Laws." *Movement Advancement Project*, 23 Feb. 2017, lgbtmap.org. Accessed 17 Jan. 2019.

8. Susan Milligan. "Isolated and Left Behind." *U.S. News & World Report*, 16 July 2018, usnews.com. Accessed 17 Jan. 2019.

CHAPTER 5. ECONOMIC CHALLENGES

1. Human Rights Campaign. "Employment." *State Maps of Laws & Policies*, 11 Jan. 2019, hrc.org. Accessed 17 Jan. 2019.

2. "The Report of the 2015 US Transgender Survey." *National Center for Transgender Equality*, Dec. 2016, transequality.org. Accessed 17 Jan. 2019.

3. Office of the Assistant Secretary for Planning and Evaluation. "2015 Poverty Guidelines." *US Department of Health and Human Services*, 3 Sept. 2015, aspe.hhs.gov. Accessed 17 Jan. 2019.

4. "The Report of the 2015 US Transgender Survey."

5. Robert Balfanz and Vaughan Byrnes. "The Importance of Being in School." *Education Digest*, vol. 78, no. 2, Oct. 2012. 4–9.

6. Anna North. "Can Transgender Students Go to Women's Colleges?" *Vox*, 22 Sept. 2017, vox.com. Accessed 17 Jan. 2019.

7. Leila Ettachfini. "The Deadly Reality for Transgender Students Facing Discrimination in School." *Broadly*, 20 Nov. 2016, broadly.vice.com. Accessed 17 Jan. 2019.

8. "2015 National School Climate Survey." *GLSEN*, 2016, glsen.org. Accessed 17 Jan. 2019.

9. Movement Advancement Project. "Non-Discrimination Laws: Employment." *Movement Advancement Project*, 8 Feb. 2019, lgbtmap.org. Accessed 11 Feb. 2019.

10. "Know Your Rights: Title VII of the Civil Rights Act of 1964." *American Association of University Women*, n.d., aauw.org. Accessed 17 Jan. 2019.

11. "Preventing Employment Discrimination against Lesbian, Gay, Bisexual, or Transgender Workers." *US Equal Employment Opportunity Commission*, n.d., eeoc.gov. Accessed 17 Jan. 2019.

12. Kevin Johnson. "Jeff Sessions: Transgender People Not Protected from Workplace Discrimination." *USA Today*, 5 Oct. 2017, usatoday.com. Accessed 17 Jan. 2019.

SOURCE NOTES
CONTINUED

13. "The Report of the 2015 US Transgender Survey."

14. "The Report of the 2015 US Transgender Survey."

15. "The Report of the 2015 US Transgender Survey."

16. Cass Averill. "Transgender Today: Cass Averill." *New York Times*, 2015, nytimes.com. Accessed 17 Jan. 2019.

17. "The Report of the 2015 US Transgender Survey."

18. Susan Milligan. "A Place to Call Home." *U.S. News & World Report*, 29 Sept. 2017, usnews.com. Accessed 17 Jan. 2019.

19. "The Report of the 2015 US Transgender Survey."

20. "Colleges and University That Provide Gender-Inclusive Housing." *Campus Pride*, n.d., campuspride.org. Accessed 17 Jan. 2019.

21. "The Report of the 2015 US Transgender Survey."

22. Elly Belle. "What Trying to Access Health Care Is Like for Transgender and Gender-Nonconforming People." *Teen Vogue*, 24 Oct. 2018, teenvogue.com. Accessed 19 Jan. 2019.

23. Susmita Baral. "What It's Like Being Transgender in the Emergency Room." *National Geographic*, 19 Mar. 2018, news.nationalgeographic.com. Accessed 17 Jan. 2019.

24. "The Report of the 2015 US Transgender Survey."

25. "Sex Reassignment Surgery Cost." *CostHelper Health*, n.d., health.costhelper.com. Accessed 17 Jan. 2019.

CHAPTER 6. HEALTH AND SAFETY CHALLENGES

1. Susan Milligan. "Isolated and Left Behind." *U.S. News & World Report*, 16 July 2018, usnews.com. Accessed 17 Jan. 2019.

2. "The Report of the 2015 US Transgender Survey." *National Center for Transgender Equality*, Dec. 2016, transequality.org. Accessed 17 Jan. 2019.

3. "The Report of the 2015 US Transgender Survey."

4. Maggie Astor. "Violence against Transgender People Is on the Rise, Advocates Say." *Boston Globe*, 10 Nov. 2017, bostonglobe.com. Accessed 17 Jan. 2019.

5. Trudy Ring. "These Are the Trans People Killed in 2018." *Advocate*, 7 Dec. 2018, advocate.com. Accessed 17 Jan. 2019.

6. Karen Kaplan. "Being Transgender in America May Be Hazardous to Your Health, Study Shows." *Los Angeles Times*, 30 May 2017, latimes.com. Accessed 17 Jan. 2019.

7. "Violence against the Transgender Community in 2018." *Human Rights Campaign*, n.d., hrc.org. Accessed 17 Jan. 2019.

8. LA Johnson and Clare Lombardo. "Transgender Teachers: In Their Own Voices." *NPR*, 18 Mar. 2018, npr.org. Accessed 17 Jan. 2019.

9. Amanda Holpuch. "Trans Children Allowed to Express Identity Have 'Good Mental Health.'" *Guardian*, 26 Feb. 2016, theguardian.com. Accessed 17 Jan. 2019.

10. Katherine Schrieber and Heather Hausenblas. "Why Transgender People Experience More Mental Health Issues." *Psychology Today*, 6 Dec. 2016, psychologytoday.com. Accessed 17 Jan. 2019.

11. Kaplan, "Being Transgender in America."

12. "The Report of the 2015 US Transgender Survey."

13. Chris. "Transgender Today: Chris." *New York Times*, 2015, nytimes.com. Accessed 17 Jan. 2019.

14. "The Report of the 2015 US Transgender Survey."

15. Medardo Perez. "Transgender Students Face Higher Rates of Substance Abuse, Study Finds." *NBC News*, 18 Aug. 2017, nbcnews.com. Accessed 17 Jan. 2019.

CHAPTER 7. TRANS PEOPLE IN THE MEDIA

1. Joanne Meyerowitz. *How Sex Changed: A History of Transsexuality in the United States*. Harvard UP, 2002. 1.

2. Simon Hattenstone. "Janet Mock: 'I'd Never Seen a Young Trans Woman Who Was Thriving in the World—I Was Looking for That." *Guardian*, 15 Apr. 2018, theguardian.com. Accessed 17 Jan. 2019.

3. "Victims or Villains: Examining Ten Years of Transgender Images on Television." *GLAAD*, n.d., glaad.org. Accessed 17 Jan. 2019.

4. Catherine Gee. "*Orange Is the New Black* Star Laverne Cox: 'Why Do People Want to Murder Us? Because We're Trans and Black.'" *Telegraph*, 8 June 2017, telegraph.co.uk. Accessed 17 Jan. 2019.

5. @Caitlyn_Jenner. "Well @realDonaldTrump, from one Republican to another, this is a disaster. . ." *Twitter*, 23 Feb. 2017, 5:18 p.m. twitter.com. Accessed 17 Jan. 2019.

6. Ramin Setoodeh. "How Caitlyn Jenner Is Secretly Fighting Trump's White House on Transgender Rights." *Variety*, 2018, variety.com. Accessed 17 Jan. 2019.

7. Nina Metz. "Why Trans Actors Should Be Cast in Trans Roles." *Chicago Tribune*, 13 July 2018, chicagotribune.com. Accessed 18 Jan. 2019.

8. Adrienne Shaw and Elizaveta Friesem. "Where Is the Queerness in Games?" *International Journal of Communication*, vol. 10, 2016. 3877–3889.

9. Elly Belle. "'Rise' Actor Ellie Desautels Opened Up about Representation of Transgender People on TV." *Teen Vogue*, 14 Mar. 2018, teenvogue.com. Accessed 18 Jan. 2019.

10. Megan Tady. "Being Transgender in American Media." *FAIR*, June 2012, fair.org. Accessed 18 Jan. 2019.

11. Neal Hall. "Transgender Beauty Queen Jenna Talackova Has a Boyfriend, Hopes to Have Children." *Vancouver Sun*, 9 Apr. 2012, vancouversun.com. Accessed 18 Jan. 2019.

12. Arin Andrews. *Some Assembly Required*. Simon, 2015. 238, 247.

CHAPTER 8. THE FUTURE OF TRANSGENDER EQUALITY

1. Aleksandra Sandstrom. "Religious Groups' Policies on Transgender Members Vary Widely." *Pew Research Center*, 2 Dec. 2015, pewresearch.org. Accessed 18 Jan. 2019.

2. Pew Research Center. "Chapter 6: Religion." *A Survey of LGBT Americans*, Pew Research Center, 13 June 2013, pewsocialtrends.org. Accessed 18 Jan. 2019.

3. Susan Milligan. "Isolated and Left Behind." *U.S. News & World Report*, 16 July 2018, usnews.com. Accessed 17 Jan. 2019.

4. "Know Your Rights: Public Accommodations." *National Center for Transgender Equality*, n.d., transequality.org. Accessed 18 Jan. 2019.

5. Kara Milstein, Katy Steinmetz, and Kim Bubello. "I Will Forever Be an American Soldier." *Time*, n.d., time.com. Accessed 18 Jan. 2019.

6. "Gender and Sexuality Alliances." *GLSEN*, n.d., glsen.org. Accessed 18 Jan. 2019.

7. Bronwyn Isaac. "How Young Doctors Are De-Bunking Transphobia in Medicine." *Bustle*, 26 June 2017, bustle.com. Accessed 18 Jan. 2019.

8. "Rain Dove: New York's Androgynous Supermodel." *YouTube*, uploaded by Bustle, 9 Sept. 2018, youtube.com. Accessed 18 Jan. 2019.

INDEX

ABOUT THE AUTHORS

DUCHESS HARRIS, JD, PHD

Dr. Harris is a professor of American Studies at Macalester College and curator of the Duchess Harris Collection of ABDO books. She is also the coauthor of the titles in the collection, which features popular selections such as *Hidden Human Computers: The Black Women of NASA* and series including News Literacy and Being Female in America.

Before working with ABDO, Dr. Harris authored several other books on the topics of race, culture, and American history. She served as an associate editor for *Litigation News*, the American Bar Association Section of Litigation's quarterly flagship publication, and was the first editor in chief of *Law Raza*, an interactive online journal covering race and the law, published at William Mitchell College of Law. She has earned a PhD in American Studies from the University of Minnesota and a JD from William Mitchell College of Law.

KRISTIN MARCINIAK

Kristin Marciniak lives in Overland Park, Kansas, with her husband, son, and a wacky golden retriever. A graduate of the University of Missouri School of Journalism, Kristin still can't believe she gets to write every day. She fills her free time with sewing, knitting, reading, and roller skating.